ADVANCE PRAISE FOR

THE INTEGRITY GAME

The Integrity Game's comparisons and thought-provoking questions can relate to anyone who has struggled with setting or reaching personal and professional goals in life. Easy to assimilate and reflective of so many similar challenges we have all experienced, this book pulls it all together with a resounding and satisfying feeling of an accomplished journey traveled.

Colin Stowell, Fire Chief
Large Metropolitan Department

The Integrity Game is cleverly written in a baseball setting to help a person discover or refine their purpose. There are many ah-ha moments in the journey of Ally and Luke that the author brilliantly integrates with the concepts and processes of The Integrity Game.

Ron Cho, Director of Operations,
The Chord Group

I want each and every WTN client to play the Integrity Game. I have seen the enormous benefit it brings to our clients' teams in terms of enhanced civility, teamwork, communication, and work performance.

Kit Goldman, President and Founder
Workplace Training Network, Inc.

This book is clearly about Mentorship and possibly Leadership. It is remarkably well written!

Ajay Gupta, Senior Partner
Gupta, Evans and Associates, PC

The Integrity Game brings so many things together in such a subtle way that it seems like you are sitting with friends, listening and learning. Jeff is a master communicator, and his GAME is strong—his integrity is unmatched.

Dave Chametsky, Author, *Peace, Love and Bring a Bat*

The Integrity Game is a brilliantly written story that drives home the idea that you need to have integrity in all areas of your life to truly have alignment, happiness, and success. You will take away some amazing lessons from this playbook written by a coach that shows you how to hit a homerun in life.

Michele Lee Malo, The Change CEO

A simple yet insightful and inspiring read that brought me back to my center. This book serves as a reminder to define your true north and create the mental structure needed to guide the way.

Jamar Williams, Founder and CEO, PromoDrone

The whole package really brings integrity alive and, certainly from my perspective, has been written in such a way that it just makes me WANT to get in and play EVERY DAY! The journey of The Integrity Game is clear, simple and can be applied to any situation with incredible results.

Sue Mathieson, The CEO Saver and
National Business Development Manager, Lexplore, PTY Ltd.
Melbourne, Australia

…Such an enjoyable read that it matters not if you understand anything about baseball. The Integrity Game contains some of the best lessons you will ever learn in life.

Michael James
Writer, Real Estate Investor

Jeff Klubeck walks the walk, and The Integrity Game is a recipe for living your best life, too! Jeff distills the formula for how to approach your daily mindset to not only achieve your goals but also be a powerful catalyst to help others reach theirs.

Brian Traichel, Master LinkedIn Trainer

Jeff deftly uses baseball to foster introspection to help you reach your potential. Our nation would no doubt be a better place if The Integrity Game were to become our National Pastime.

Rich Grayson

Integrity comes in many shapes and forms, and this book provides you with the tools you need to build a foundation for success. I recommend it to those who are looking to take their life and business to new heights.

Damien Elston, Founder, Capital Fitness

I really enjoyed this read! Great way to introduce how you use Integrity in your coaching process – and take it from a nebulous very, very subjective concept to a concrete actionable state of being. All that and I'm not even a baseball fan!

Milly Christman, Marathon Growth Management

This book is a little snippet of Jeff's commitment to bring honor and integrity into this world and to raise up to make a difference for every human being he meets, just as Terry does with Luke in this sweet story.

Meg Fritton, Interior Design, Executive Coach

THE
INTEGRITY
GAME

MOTIVATION + ACCOUNTABILITY = RESULTS!

JEFFREY KLUBECK

THE INTEGRITY GAME

Motivation + Accountability = Results!

Jeffrey Klubeck

COPYRIGHT © 2022

ISBN 978-1-7330862-6-4

Cover design by Sean O'Connor

OhSeeDesign@gmail.com

Printed in the United States of America

CONTENTS

DEDICATIONS

First and foremost, to Mary Ann. When people ask me what I do for a living, I always say that I "wake up every day and figure out how I am going to deserve my wife and kids!" All three of our kids are partially represented by some characters in this book ... but there ARE NO KIDS ... there IS NO BOOK or anything else without you, my friend, partner, lover, wife, and, as you like to playfully remind me and others in my world that you meet. my coach! ☺

Traditionally, a marriage *"integrates"* previously single partners *and* *"transforms"* then into *a union*. In a world where over 50% disintegrate into divorce, our 30+ years of being in love and 20+ years of marriage have the *"structural integrity"* that has withstood EVERY outside force to *remain standing!* At core, we are strongly *integrated by our love* (our laces!) and will remain so until death do us part. That's what we said we'd do ... that's what we've done ... that's what we'll continue to do!

For my part, will you, Mary Ann, also let me say that IF IT WEREN'T for you and how hard I believe I need to work ... how "good" I think I need to be ... how many people I think I need to help JUST to feel like I deserve you, my life could very easily have gone down a much darker and destructive path.

In many ways, your love has saved me from my "station" in this life.

Your love has motivated me to GET out of my own way … to BE Accountable and to LIVE with greater integrity tomorrow than I did yesterday. I do not believe that I would be capable of playing The Integrity Game with anyone else. It's you … it has always been you … it will always be YOU, Mary Ann! Thanks, Coach! ☺

Second, in eternal gratitude and loving memory for Coach Gene Higgs who *re-integrated* with his maker in 2020, I also dedicate this book to his wife, Jacqueline, and the Higgs family, who treated mine as theirs all through the "Little League years" and since. We are all destined for a big pool party in the sky. Gene, once again, has given of himself to lead the way and get everything ready for us. I believe he would have LOVED this book, and I sure hope you do, too!

Let's play…

FOREWORD

In *The Integrity Game*, Executive Coach Jeff Klubeck has hit a homerun, pun intended! His allegory weaves the great game of baseball with how we can all fulfill the purpose that we were put on this earth to accomplish and is a wonderful story that should resonate with everyone, baseball fan or otherwise.

The story centers on a young man named Luke, a concessionaire at a baseball stadium, who struggles to find his way in the world, partly because of his own stubbornness and poor attitude but also because no one has ever taken the time to mentor him. This is where the protagonist, Terry, enters the story, a wise sage who decides that Luke is worth taking the time to help.

The Integrity Game is written effusively and kind-heartedly—to anyone who knows Jeff, this should come as no surprise. It has been proven scientifically that it is impossible to have a bad day when you are around Jeff Klubeck. From the first time he greets you, he surrounds you with his warmth, his authenticity, but most of all, you know deep down in your soul that he cares very deeply for you and wants absolutely nothing but the best for you.

Perhaps, it has also been proven that if you are out of integrity, Jeff is very likely to find a way to call you on it ... again, always for your own good and sometimes at his own expense! Not everyone gets it.

Luke started playing along early in the book (who wouldn't after watching Susan Sarandon in *Bull Durham*?), but some people never come around to The Integrity Game Jeff is always encouraging us to play.

I often joke that if you hang around long enough, you end up with an impressive sounding bio. While I have done a lot of different things in my career (Retired Navy Rear Admiral, Entrepreneur, Small Business Owner, Real Estate Investor, Adjunct Professor, Football Coach), it all comes back to leadership, which is my life's passion. And to be a great leader, you must love people, and that is what Jeff and I share—a deep love of people and a hunger to see them succeed.

I first met Jeff when he started coaching an employee of mine. When my employee urged me to meet Jeff, I had never met an Executive Coach and really didn't know what to expect. From that day forward, I have considered Jeff a mentor, as well as a friend. Whenever I would run into a business issue, my first thought was (and is), *I wonder what Jeff would think about this situation?* He has helped me innumerable times ,and what is exciting for me is that with the publication of *The Integrity Game*, more people will be exposed to Jeff's methodology and have the opportunity to become better people and contributors to our society—Lord knows we need it right now.

James McNeal, Retired Rear Admiral
US Navy

INTRODUCTION

Welcome to The Integrity Game! From the very first word, the process of writing this book has been a labor of love—and for good reason, because it *integrates* the things that are most important to me: my profession, my passion/purpose, my love for my family, and, yes, the greatest sport of all time, baseball.

I have always felt that personal/professional growth is "hard enough" without complicating it even more with over-done diagrams, models, stuffy/academic language, intense meta-data, and a host of other delivery mechanisms that can be off-putting.

Thus, my first hope for The Integrity Game® is that you appreciate the simplicity of the parable and see it as the "trojan horse" for arguably complex thoughts I intend to inspire on the topic of integrity.

My second hope is that you see pieces of yourself in any (or perhaps all) of the book's characters … I hope that in "seeing" Luke or Ally or Terry or TJ or Bubba, you are ultimately able to *look within!*

In my experience, *the word "integrity"* (like accountability, parenting, or driving) is a term that *is most often used when someone is accusing someone ELSE of being poor at it,* as if they are fine/perfect. I believe we are usually guilty of what we accuse others of doing or being, and *one of the reasons it is so easy to notice a lack of integrity in others is because of how much room we have to improve our own.* It's always easier to accuse others than look within. So, as one of my mentors, Brian Tracy, would say, "Eat that frog!" and make the hardest thing to do (looking within) your number one priority when it comes to improving your ability to hold others accountable—it starts with our own accountability.

In much the same way you cannot love others unless you love yourself, you cannot hold others accountable unless you have the experience in your own life of being held accountable. *The question of WHAT we (want, need, should, must) be held accountable TO is the question this book attempts to answer!*

My third hope, then, is that I literally EXPAND your understanding of integrity in such a way that you SEEK to be held accountable to increasing your own integrity.

In fact, I hereby declare my belief that the subject of ALL accountability is integrity … *that anything anyone can ever be held accountable to will always be some sort of "integration" between one thing and another.*

Most of the time, it is our word with our behavior—many people are ready to add values, morals, or ethics into the equation. Still, a lot of people have "half a loaf" understanding when it comes to integrity. When I am training independent coaches and managers/directors of organizations, *I am always teaching people to focus on the word "integration" when it comes to an understanding of integrity— where one thing comes together with another thing.*

When I deliver The Integrity Game® keynote speeches, I always ask the audience to help me answer the question, "What IS Integrity?"

and I ALWAYS get two answers …I always get the same two answers. I never do NOT get both of these answers, and whenever people attempt to offer a third answer, they are really just restating one of these two basic answers/understandings of what integrity is:

- Doing what you said you are going to do (bonus for adding "when you said you are going to do it!") or "be your word," in short.

- Do the same thing when nobody is watching that you would do when someone IS watching! Or, in short, to "be honest."

What I love about both of these answers is how they allow me to introduce the concept of "integration" to our understanding— meaning, w*hen we DO what we SAID we would do, our behavior is integrated with our word.* And *when we behave consistent regardless of who's watching, we have integrated our behavior with our values/morals/ethics.*

In both cases, we can see the "integration" … the coming together of one thing (our word or values) with another (our behavior!). And, in both cases, *it is OUR BEHAVIOR (not our words or professed values/ethics but literally what we DO) that is the "evidence of our integrity!"* We begin to claim integrity as SOON as our behavior "comes together" with our word or values.

Humor me a bit here, DESPITE the fact that both words (Integrity and Integration) start with the same six letters, if I asked a million people what the definition of integrity is, and not a single answer would include the word "integration." I have seen the looks on faces in my audience when I point this out … I hope you just felt "that face" privately! ☺

So, I selfishly love those two answers because of the opportunity it gives me to introduce "integration" into the world's understanding of integrity.

What I also love about those two answers is the way I can challenge them as "not enough" when it comes to integrity. For example, if I said I was going to commit a crime and then I DID commit a crime, would I be able to say I have integrity? If I refuse to practice personal hygiene when people are watching, will I have integrity if I refuse to practice personal hygiene when no one is watching?

In these two examples of "integrating" word with behavior (crime) or values with behavior (hygiene), there IS integration, but you would cringe if I claimed to have Integrity based on those examples. My fourth and final hope for this book is that *you want to know what else I believe we need to "integrate" in order to have/claim greater integrity.* This book introduces my 10-point model for accountability that I call The Integrity Game®! The read is quick and easy … a single-player game in the form of a parable set to baseball.

In this book, you'll meet Luke, a hot dog vendor who is out of integrity in his career and his life. I invite you to follow his journey of growth as he discovers his gifts and purpose and implements the principles that put him on the path of success. Along the way, you'll meet Terry, a season ticket holder, mentor, and coach, who, like me, is an imperfect baseball dad who struggles and strives to wear a badge of integrity with pride. TJ, his son, is a rookie whose character was inspired by my son, AJ. Ally, a personable young woman who knows what she wants and is motivated to make it happen, is much like my daughter, Abigail. And last, but most definitely not least, I introduce a new hero, one who is committed to making the world a better place, like my son, Brody, fondly known as "Bubba."

Life is not a spectator sport. We don't have to settle for walking the bases or simply going through the motions. With the Integrity Game in play, we'll be ready to step up to the plate and swing for the fences.

Let the Integrity Game begin!

1

MEET THE PLAYERS

 Da-da-da-da-da-daaa …

"Charge!" the crowd roared in reply to the organ's rally call.

It was the bottom of the ninth inning at Victor Stadium, and the crowd was on its feet, hoping for that one run that would tie the game and send the ball game into extra innings … or better, two runs for a "walk off" win! The sound was deafening as the batter approached the plate, a rookie who had recently been called up from Triple A— now finding himself one of the team's last two shots at scoring a much-needed run.

"Come on, TJ," a middle-aged man sitting on an aisle seat in a shaded row at the top of his section said, almost to himself, "You can do it!"

The first pitch crossed the plate, and the umpire's fist signaled strike one. A swing and a miss made the count 0 and 2.

"Shorten everything, son. Choke up and protect. Watch for off-speed. Make him work for it," the man whispered encouragement … just as he had when he volunteered as a coach for his son's team during the Little League days …

Almost as if the batter had heard the man's advice, he defensively swung at the next pitch trying to foul it off when, suddenly, the ball took a nosedive into the dirt that caused a hard bounce over the catcher's head.

A wild pitch! The crowd was on its feet again as the batter flung his bat and raced toward first base on the "swinging" dropped third strike...

"Safe!" signaled the first base umpire.

"Atta boy, TJ!" the man exclaimed, this time letting his voice be heard among the crowd.

"Oh, great. Leave it to the rookie to make sure we don't get out of here at a decent hour," a sandy-haired vendor moaned to a female coworker from behind the rail. His words were spoken a little louder than intended—just loud enough that they caught the attention of the middle-aged man who stood to their right. Surprised to hear the vendor actually root against the home team, the fan refused to let it wane his enthusiasm.

"Luke and Ally, if we go into extra innings, I need you to stick around," said a female voice over the walkie talkie.

"Are you kidding me!" exclaimed the male vendor.

"C'mon, Luke, it'll give us a chance to make a few more bucks. Weren't you just complaining about not getting enough tips?" the female, a long-haired brunette, spoke.

"But it's Friday night. Ally, I'm supposed to meet up with the guys after the game. This happens every time I have plans. It's like our boss is out to get me," Luke complained.

"No, she's not. You heard her—it's our turn. We might as well make the best of it and get ready to restock," Ally said as she walked toward the concourse.

Muttering something unintelligible under his breath, Luke turned toward the field. Two outs, with a runner on first, and the count was 3 and 1. Just as the pitcher released the ball, the runner on first took off for second. The catcher fired the ball to the second baseman, and to the crowd's disapproval, the runner was called out.

"All right!" Luke yelled.

Again, the man glanced at the vendor, surprised that he was so vocal about hoping that the home team would lose.

"The play is under review," the announcer reported over the loudspeakers.

"Of course it is! Let's just drag this on as long as we can," Luke uttered out loud, refusing to move from the spot where he'd been standing since the beginning of the inning.

Ignoring the vendor's snide comments, the man joined the crowd in watching the replay on the jumbotron. From another angle, the runner was clearly safe and the call was reversed, which sparked the crowd's enthusiasm once again.

"Get a life, people. It's just a game," muttered the vendor.

As the opposing manager emerged from the dugout for a mound visit with the count now 3 balls, 2 strikes, with one out and the rookie on second.

"Excuse me," the man said to the vendor, believing a pitching change was coming. "I couldn't help but overhearing. I take it you're not a Victors fan?"

"Me? I'm a fan, but it's really not that big of a deal. I just wish they'd hurry up and win or hurry up and lose. I've got things to do," Luke replied.

"Hmm, must be really important things you have to do—I mean, to stand among all of your customers and openly root for their team to lose ... not to mention, specifically, the rookie who probably needs our support as much as anyone on the team right now," the man pointed out.

"Hey, you have no clue what you're talking about. Unlike you, I'm here for every game, win or lose. My life revolves around baseball, but baseball isn't everything to everybody," Luke pointed out.

"I might not know what you're talking about," the man admitted. "But I do know a few things. For starters, to some people, baseball is a lot more than *just* a ballgame. It's their dream, their future, their career. It's part of their life, their family, and their traditions. And in case you forgot, it's also a livelihood for the owners and staff—even vendors, like you. So, do you mind if I ask why you don't seem to like your job?"

"Maybe I would if things were different," Luke replied.

"Like what things?"

"Like not having to give up Friday night with the guys. Like actually bringing home some decent tips. Like having a boss who would give me a good section once in a while. And having a little fun on the job wouldn't hurt," Luke said, rattling off his complaints.

"I guess that is a lot of 'things' not to like. It seems to me that perhaps you didn't come to this job prepared to play."

"What do you mean?"

A roar from the crowd interrupted their conversation, and the men turned toward the field to see the mound visit had ended and the 3-2 pitch was a fly ball into deep left field, where to the fans' disappointment, it was caught at the fence.

There were two outs, the rookie had to stay on second, and the next hitter was the Victors' all-star left-handed first baseman. Again, the opposing manager walked onto the field to make a pitching change, going with a left-hander of his own to play the percentages of a favorable lefty-lefty matchup.

Knowing he had another two minutes while the new pitcher warmed up, the man turned back to an even more upset Luke and resumed, "Hey, man, it doesn't get more exciting than this ... if you don't like your job, what are you doing about it, other than complaining?"

"Nothing. There's nothing I can do. Nobody would listen if I said anything, so why even bother?"

"Oh, I see. So, it's better to complain about everything in the world, rather than doing anything about your own world?"

"Hey, that's not fair. You don't even know me ..."

"You're right, I don't. But I've met people like you, and from experience, it isn't just this job you are unhappy with. I'd bet you have something to complain about in ALL the areas of your life ...even the friends you are so eager to hang out with after the game ... I'll bet you complain about them from time to time, too, right? But they are your friends, and there is nothing you can do about them, right?

"You see, if I am right," the man continued, "then I don't think you can be happy here ... or anywhere, for that matter."

"What are you talking about?" Luke asked.

"I'd be happy to tell you. but first, let me ask you just one more question: Do you believe you have integrity?"

"Sure," Luke answered.

"If you promise not to shoot the messenger, I'll beg to differ, young man. And it's not that you don't have 'any' integrity, but the truth is that we are all out of integrity on some level. That includes me, and that's okay because I believe we never have 100 percent integrity until we die … until we are 're-integrated' with our maker. Until then, we're all human and, yes, we are all flawed … that includes me, and it certainly includes you!"

"What's integrity got to do with anything?" Luke asked.

"Well, think about things like parenting or driving a car if you don't have kids –there are things we all think WE are good at but everyone ELSE sucks at it. The same is true with your job. Your boss isn't fair. The fans are cheap. I get it. But I also know that the person who is complaining and accusing others of being out of integrity is usually the person who is actually out of integrity. It's not a judgement, just a fact that it is easier to complain about others than it is to take action and responsibility for ourselves."

"Your name is Luke, right?" the man confirmed.

"Right."

"Nice to meet you, Luke. I'm Terry," the man offered. "For example, I've been standing next to you for some time now. You're complaining about not making enough money, but I haven't seen you try to sell anyone, including me, a hot dog. Why not?"

"Like I said, I'm ready to wrap things up and go home," Luke answered.

Almost as if on cue, with the pitching change (and commercial break for those that were watching at home) complete, the game resumed with the batter jumping on the first pitch and shooting a groundball just past the shortstop! The crowd went wild as the rookie, TJ, rounded third and raced home safely. The game was tied!

"HA HA! It looks like THAT's not going to happen," Terry triumphantly remarked, almost as if still cheering the clutch hit by the all-star and TJ's lightning speed.

"Luke, I need you to report *now*," came a voice over the walkie talkie.

"Looks like you've got to go, Luke. But, in all seriousness, I want you to remember that you're not complaining about a baseball game or whether your boss is playing fair. Everything you're complaining about is actually yourself and the fact that you are not winning … heck, perhaps not even playing the game of integrity. In the Integrity Game, you have to be honest with yourself. In the Integrity Game, you have to answer tough questions, make difficult decisions, and take action and responsibility for all of it! If you are tired of a life where you are constantly complaining about other people and 'things' beyond your control, and you believe you're prepared to play, then I think I can help you," the man offered.

"I can't now—didn't you hear, I have to go back to work," Luke replied.

"Oh, I know. But I'll be here until the last pitch is thrown, I assure you. And I'll be back again tomorrow."

"Oh, you have series tickets?"

"No, I'm a season ticket holder. I come to every game to support my son—he's the rookie that started this rally going," Terry smiled proudly. "In our family, baseball is much more than a game … it is a mechanism to learn about life and what separates winners from losers. And in our family, integrity is much more than something we accuse others of not having. Integrity is the standard by which the success of all our decisions and actions gets measured! If you take nothing else from our talk, take this: If anything is out of integrity, EVERYTHING is out of integrity!"

"That rookie is your son? Okay, now you've got my attention. So, integrity is really that big of a deal?" Luke asked.

"Not only is it a big deal, young man, I'd say 'it's the ONLY game in town.' I hope I get a chance to teach you how to play, but remember, you have to be honest at all times and ready to look within. You know where to find me tomorrow … and all season long!"

2

PURPOSE

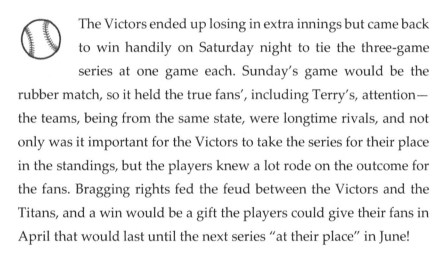The Victors ended up losing in extra innings but came back to win handily on Saturday night to tie the three-game series at one game each. Sunday's game would be the rubber match, so it held the true fans', including Terry's, attention—the teams, being from the same state, were longtime rivals, and not only was it important for the Victors to take the series for their place in the standings, but the players knew a lot rode on the outcome for the fans. Bragging rights fed the feud between the Victors and the Titans, and a win would be a gift the players could give their fans in April that would last until the next series "at their place" in June!

Adding to the rivalry was the fact that the teams were expected to compete for the Division Title all season and, early in the season, they were especially well matched for this game. Both of their pitching "Aces" (Opening Day starters) were facing each other, and their top hitters were battling each other for the early season league lead in home runs with seven each! These elements were certain to make this the game to watch, and that's what Terry did. His eyes glued to the field, he was so caught up in the game that he didn't come up for air, let alone his first trip to the bathroom, until there was a pitching change in the sixth inning with the score tied 1-1.

As he turned from his aisle seat toward the top step of his section while the team was holding batting practice, Terry noticed his new friend, Luke, who was off to the side of the concourse on one knee, tying his shoe.

"Hi there, Hot Dog!" was Terry's cheerful attempt to greet the vendor, who looked no less disgruntled than he had on Friday since the game was tied in the sixth inning and the possibility of extra innings grew higher with each pitch.

"Whatcha doin' down there … praying today's game doesn't go into extra innings, too?" Terry asked with a smile, hoping Luke would know he was just kidding and, more important, that Luke's skin was thick enough to absorb some good old-fashioned guy-to-guy rousing.

"Oh, great!" Luke replied with a tone of voice that matched Terry's playful antagonism. "It's Mr. Integrity," Luke continued, "back for another game to teach me how to sell more hot dogs … and, now, how to tie my shoes, I'm guessing?"

Super relieved that Luke was ready to both laugh at himself and also playfully fight back a bit, Terry saw an opening!

"I don't think you need help with knowing how to tie your shoes … but you might be interested in learning what shoes can teach us about integrity."

"Hey, man, I was just kidding with that Mr. Integrity thing … like you calling me Hot Dog … I wasn't asking for another lecture, just being playful."

"Relax, Luke," Terry replied assuredly. "I told you Friday that I take integrity very seriously, but I also take playfulness JUST as seriously, odd as that sounds. I am SERIOUS about having FUN, and I always try to use humor as the 'trojan horse' to get serious stuff through to people! That's why I referred to 'integrity' yesterday as 'The Integrity Game' — to make it playful, fun, less pressure, less judgmental, easier to understand and easier to act upon."

"Okay, so we're cool … good!" Luke affirmed and continued, "The truth is I probably DO want another lecture. I mean, I still don't know what you do, but it's clear to me that you are about helping or teaching people or whatever, and so far I haven't screwed up your interest in helping me … I'm just not used to people wanting to help me."

Terry smiled, it seemed, beyond ear-to-ear, and if you'd seen that smile, you'd know that Terry saw something in Luke that reminded him of himself. "Remind me one day to tell you the story about how I nearly dropped out of college but chose to receive help that was offered to me—help that hurt my pride … help that hurt my parents' pride … help that created a debt, but help I committed to repay—not just the financial part, but for the rest of my life, I'm committed to helping others in the ways that I've been helped in getting where I am now."

Luke actually saw Terry's eyes well up with tears. Then Luke thought he noticed Terry's lips tremble a bit. It was when Terry's breathing noticeably changed that Luke knew the older man had touched on a subject that triggered his emotions. Literally all the emotion of gratitude that consumed Terry at that moment was on display for Luke, non-verbally, in addition to the words Terry was able to get out.

"How about you just tell me what my shoes have to do with integrity for now?" Luke said in a super acute, well-timed delivery of comic relief.

Luke's comment allowed for a shift from Terry's emotional memories, and, also, permission for Terry to get back to the most important thing he could do for Luke: The Integrity Game!

"Okay, but you have to promise me you'll sell some darn hot dogs today, okay?" Terry playfully demanded, while bringing his own emotions back to calm. "How much time do you have right now?"

Luke replied, "I've got a few minutes yet."

"Here we go. Luke, do you see those laces on your shoe?"

"Yeah. What about them?"

"What are they doing there? Terry asked.

"Again, they're tying my shoe."

"No, you're not getting my point. Do you see how they're woven through the holes and they zig-zag and crisscross from side to side? They are integrating the left side of the shoe with the right side … you say 'tying,' but that is what YOU are doing TO the laces. What the LACES are doing TO the shoe, however, is providing integrity! By running through the holes, the laces integrate the left side with the right side … and a well-tied set of laces will KEEP the shoe 'in integrity.' Get it? Good, but why? Why integrate the left and right? Why do we lace the shoes or tie the laces at all?"

"So the shoe stays on my foot…" Luke offered in that "no duh" kind of voice that both called out the obvious but steadied himself for a "trick answer" if this was a trick question. Then he continued, "…uh, so I don't trip?" this time with a rising inflection that indicated he was asking as much as answering.

"That's one way of saying it, Luke. In fact, you are 100 percent correct. And another way of saying it is this: So, the shoe can reach its potential and DO what it was MADE to do! The shoe was made to protect your foot ... but untied, it has less of a chance of protecting your foot—even worse, if it falls off or trips and injures you! Anything out of integrity not only misses out on its own potential, but it can get in the way of others' potential, too! You go from unprotected foot, to twisted ankle, to late for work, to on the streets and homeless ALL because one thing was out of integrity: the laces! Okay, so I am exaggerating for fun, but..."

"Okay," Luke interrupted, "yeah, that's starting to make some sense, I guess ... but what's your point?" he asked.

Without missing a beat, Terry continued. "If we can increase our integrity, cinch up our integrity, we have a better chance to reach our potential and do what we're 'born to do' and live with purpose by living our purpose. Most of the people out there on the field are living their purpose. They're in integrity, doing what many of them believe they were literally born to do. I remember feeling that way about my son, TJ ... that he was born to play the game. You know, we never stopped believing he had the potential to make it to the big leagues— The Show! Now, he's here ... but I can assure you that if he were out of integrity in the classroom, in relationships, at home, or with the law, he'd have NO chance of playing pro ball!"

"Does everything revolve around baseball with you?" Luke asked defensively, as if Terry was getting closer to something Luke wasn't ready to discuss yet.

"Does *anything* revolve around baseball for you? Son, why are you here? It's obvious that you don't really want to be."

"It's a job. That's why I'm here. But it's not like I think baseball is the meaning of life or something," Luke answered.

"NOW we are getting somewhere!" Terry said with loud emphasis on the word "now" and a super warm smile that packaged the rest of his exclamation—*we are getting somewhere*!

"Uh, where?"

"Meaning of Life! You just said, it's not like you think baseball is the meaning of life … so now I get to ask you two critical questions that will set you on your way to playing The Integrity Game. You don't have to answer them now … because you can't. It will require the looking within and soul searching I mentioned Friday, But I think you are ready. Are you?"

"I think so, but you have to buy more than one hot dog if this is going to take much longer," Luke said, half joking as he suddenly showed awareness for the time and his poor sales totals.

"Ha ha …you bet. In fact, get super clear on these two questions, and I'll buy the rest of your tray to share with season-ticket holder friends in my section. Remember the tennis-shoe metaphor? The first loop we have to get our laces through is Meaning! Okay, so, here's the first question," Terry announced, pausing briefly for effect. "What IS the meaning of life? You were quick to say what you don't think it is—baseball—but how quickly would you be able to respond if someone asked, 'What IS the meaning of life?' I am not asking you to answer for everyone—just for you. In your own personal opinion, what do you believe is the meaning of life?"

"Huh? I thought we were talking about baseball or my job. What kind of question is that?" Luke asked, again a bit defensively.

"Well, we are talking about baseball. And we are talking about your job. And, I might add, we are also talking about life. It all goes back to integrity. Do you remember me touching on that briefly on Friday?" Terry asked, without waiting for an answer or even taking a breath, it seemed. "You see, it is really difficult to claim to have integrity in any area of your life if you don't have an answer to the question 'what is the meaning of life?' There has to be some foundation, some belief about what life means, which you then build or integrate into your own life, young man. Some people are out of integrity for never arriving at a meaning for life. Others are out of integrity for failing to live up to the meaning they have arrived at."

"Now, your meaning of life can come from religion, or it could be spirituality. It might be philosophical or political. It's not a test— there is no wrong or right answer here. But we all need to rely on some form of thought leadership that guides us and to help us define the meaning or meanings of life."

"Umm, I don't … I'm not sure," Luke stammered.

"It's alright. I don't expect you to have an answer to that question right away, but I can't let you go on another day without attempting to answer it. The danger is that if you don't assign a value to life—if you don't believe in a meaning to life—you will have a hard time respecting life, promoting life, actualizing life, optimizing life, and so forth. The first-responding firefighter and the armed gang member are both willing to risk their life, but they assign a completely different meaning to life that fuels their risk."

"I'm not sure I get where you're coming from, sir. Can you explain it a little better?"

"Is there any theology in your life? Maybe you grew up in a certain religion, or you subscribe to a specific philosophy. Maybe, like an old college friend I once traveled around the country with, the laws of physics are the only laws you observe," he chuckled. "Seriously, some people think the meaning of life is to fight evil, some think it is to save the planet, others think it is to discover new life, and other broad concepts like that. Remember, there is no 'right or wrong' for what you believe to be the meaning of life. I simply caution that you have something you believe versus nothing … that you have some value for life because that is the critical step toward truly cherishing your OWN life! You can arrive at meaning of life from anywhere, Luke. And, yes, it *could* even be baseball."

"Baseball?"

"Sure, baseball. I think a great example I can give you comes from Susan Sarandon's character in the movie, *Bull Durham*, where she talks about the church of baseball and demonstrates that baseball can be the source of meaning one has for life. You've seen *Bull Durham*, right?"

Without waiting for an answer, Terry continued, "And, to answer your earlier question, is baseball the meaning of MY life? Not really. I would prefer to say that I believe 'integrity' is the meaning of life … and I have found that very few things help me explain or enjoy that better than baseball!

"Baseball is a game of integrity. Everything always adds up and is accounted for … nothing and nobody hides in baseball. 'The ball will find you!' as they say, it's all out in the open. Actually, it's a brilliant and entertaining way to learn about life and success."

"Baseball isn't, itself, the meaning of life, but I do believe that very few things teach us about winning and losing in life the way the game of baseball does. It is the grand American institution. And it just happened to be Susan Sarandon who taught me there are 108 beads in a Catholic rosary and 108 stitches in a baseball. Coincidental?" Terry paused, with an inflection and a raise of the eyebrows that provoked Luke's attention.

"It's something to think about, Luke. The best advice I can give you is to turn to the major institutions that provide thought leadership for answers. And, again, baseball can be one. It doesn't matter where you find your answer, just that you do! Because without an answer, you'll be like a garden hose with no purpose or direction. Your water will run everywhere, but it will be wasted, instead of helping the right things in your life grow!"

Pausing to make sure he had the young man's attention, Terry continued.

"Is the meaning of life to have a family and provide for them? Is the meaning of life to prosper and grow? Is the meaning of life to love and help one another? Or, Luke, is the meaning of life to get through the day so you can get out of here? I can't answer those questions for you, but if you reflect on them, you can find your answer," the season ticket holder said.

"That's kind of deep," the vendor said.

"Ha ha ... actually, it's broad! My NEXT question is the deep one!"

"Uh, oh..."

Not letting Luke fully brace himself, Terry launched question number two, "What is the meaning of YOUR life? Not all of life—just YOURS! Why are YOU here ... on this planet ... with whatever gifts and circumstances you've been given? Luke, what is *your* purpose?

We know the shoe is made to protect a foot, but what about *you*? Why were you made?"

"Most people have trouble declaring their purpose, choosing their purpose, committing to a purpose, or sacrificing for a purpose. They are afraid of missing out on other pursuits. or they are afraid of the hard work involved to be true to a purpose. Some people choose destructive purposes and/or fail to change when their behaviors no longer serve their purpose. To me, the worst is failing to either choose, declare, or know a purpose at all. You might be able to tie a shoe without lacing the top left hole, but I will always recommend starting there—top left—Purpose!

"Why does life exist? Why does Luke's life exist? Got it? Those are the two questions … repeat them back to me, and I'll buy the rest of the hot dogs in your tray!"

"What is the meaning of life? What is the meaning of MY life?" Luke repeated in his own words, showing Terry that he was really listening!

"Bravo or, close enough, I mean!" Terry chuckled. "Now, to be a man of my word and protect MY integrity, how much for the rest of those hot dogs, Hot Dog!?"

"$81," Luke responded almost before Terry was done asking.

"How do you know that? We haven't even counted how many hot dogs are left," asked Terry.

"There are 17 left at $4.75 each, and that makes $81 even. Well, 80.75 to be exact, but I figured you were good for at least a 25-cent tip," Luke qualified.

"Do you sell 17 hot dogs at a time very often, or did you just calculate that in your head?"

"It's pretty easy to figure out. I know how many dogs I start with … I know what I pay for them and how much I make per dog based on the $4.75 sale price—that's before tips. I always know exactly how many dogs I have at all times, so getting to the starting versus current value of my tray at any time is a calculation I can make from several directions! I'm telling you, it's $80.75 … count 'em!"

"I believe you, Luke," Terry affirmed, while trying to hide his mild bewilderment at Luke's math. "Please, keep the change," he concluded, handing Luke a $100 bill. "If I don't see you before I leave, keep thinking about those two questions, and I'll see you at the next series!"

Terry returned to his section a hero with more hot dogs than he could give away. "A lot of people say no at first just to be polite," Terry would say when a fellow season ticket holder would refuse the offer, but Terry would continue, "It's actually a form of dishonesty to refuse a free hot dog at a baseball game…" and then people would accept with a chuckle.

The Victors went on to win the game 4-2, giving them the series win over the Titans, two games to one. Terry's son, TJ, played well when getting opportunities all weekend. He wasn't a starter yet, but he was making a name for himself as a fan favorite with his speed on the basepaths late in close ball games.

On his way out of the stadium, Terry saw Luke again.

"Great game and great talk today! I'm sure you're ready to get out of here. You going to grab a cold one with your buddies?"

"I don't think so. I think I'm going to stay home tonight and watch a movie," Luke said.

That night, Luke sat on the sofa and scrolled through the television screen until he found the on-demand movie he was looking for. As the *Bull Durham* title scrolled across the screen and the opening monologue began, he leaned forward to listen closely to Susan Sarandon's character, Annie Savoy, integrate love, spirituality, and baseball into her life's meaning:

> *I believe in the Church of Baseball. I've tried all the major religions, and most of the minor ones. I've worshipped Buddha, Allah, Brahma, Vishnu, Siva, trees, mushrooms, and Isadora Duncan. I know things. For instance, there are 108 beads in a Catholic rosary, and there are 108 stitches in a baseball. When I learned that, I gave Jesus a chance. But it just didn't work out between us. The Lord laid too much guilt on me. I prefer metaphysics to theology. You see, there's no guilt in baseball, and it's never boring which makes it ... like making love ... [it's] like hitting a baseball: you just gotta relax and concentrate. You see, there's a certain amount of life wisdom I give these boys. I can expand their minds. Sometimes when I got a ballplayer alone, I'll just read Emily Dickinson or Walt Whitman to him, and the guys are so sweet, they always stay and listen...I make them feel confident, and they make me feel safe, and pretty. 'Course, what I give them lasts a lifetime; what they give me lasts 142 games. Sometimes it seems like a bad trade. But bad trades are part of baseball—now, who can forget Frank Robinson for Milt Pappas, for God's sake? It's a long season and you gotta trust it. I've tried*

'em all, I really have, and the only church that truly feeds the soul, day in, day out, is the Church of Baseball.[1]

As the credits rolled nearly two hours later, a realization came to Luke. Annie Savoy was right. The season ticket holder was right. Baseball and life were very much alike, and the players in both were playing the same game—The Integrity Game!

---

[1] *Bull Durham (1988)*, Screenwriter(s): Ron Shelton. Orion Pictures, https://en.wikipedia.org/wiki/Bull_Durham

3

GIFTS

It was the last game before the Victors went on the road in May, and Terry relished every minute of it. After winning the weekend series against the rival Titans, the winning continued against the overmatched Blue Devils on Monday and Tuesday, giving the Victors a chance for the series sweep before leaving town!

Having season tickets was great, and Terry made every effort to watch all the home games from the stands. Grateful that his business allowed him the flexibility to schedule his work around his family, he missed the atmosphere when the team was away. While he could always watch those games on TV, it lacked the excitement and energy of being in the stands with the fans and feeling like a genuine part of the game.

The middle of the third inning, with the bottom of the Victors batting order due up, was the perfect opportunity to grab a bite to eat and something to drink. However, quickly scanning the area, Terry didn't see any vendors.

Oh, well, if they won't come to me, I guess I'll have to go to them, he thought as he walked to the concourse.

As one might expect, the concourse was packed. The lines were three or four wide and at least eight people deep as he walked by pizza, burger, and taco booths. From the sideline, he watched to see which lines were moving fastest when Luke walked by.

"Hey, Hot Dog! Are you hiding from me?" he jested.

"Uh, no. I'm working, remember?" Luke countered.

They moved out of the busy hallway and stood up against a concrete wall away from the noise of the hungry fans. Terry hoped Luke could take some time for a proper conversation.

"Okay, just wondered" Terry said, "Haven't seen you all game … in fact, I haven't seen you since Sunday. They got you working in a different section or something?"

"No. They're just keeping me busy out there. You know how it is," Luke explained.

"Not really. So, you must be crushing it today then. Good to hear! We just might make a hot dog salesman out of you yet!"

"C'mon, selling hot dogs isn't anyone's dream job. It's certainly not mine," Luke retorted.

"Fair enough. So, what *is* your dream job?"

"Who knows," the young man shrugged. "My head is still spinning trying to answer the last two questions you asked me!"

"Hey, now, I'm trying to help. Did you come up with any possible answers? Remember, there's no right or wrong, but if you don't know what your life means, chances are greater that you'll waste it — your life, that is. It's *worth* thinking about," Terry said, this time with compassion.

"A little," Luke admitted, "but it's a lot to consider, and I haven't had the time."

"Or the desire, perhaps?" Terry asked, raising his eyebrows. "I know it seems like work, and that's a four-letter word to some people, but it's work that pays off big time in the long run, I assure you. But enough about that … how're you liking the game? I'm really liking the relief pitcher we just called up. What an arm! That kid is going to do great things with his gift."

"Maybe," agreed Luke. "It's only his first game, so we don't know yet if it's luck or talent."

"Ever the skeptic, huh. Well, I'm going on record to say that he's got a *gift*," Terry remarked.

"Maybe it's not a gift. Maybe his mommy and daddy paid out the nose to give him private pitching lessons since he was old enough to walk. Maybe that's more like it," Luke surmised.

"A gift is a gift, regardless of whether it comes naturally at birth or if it's given to us by another person or even self-made … doesn't matter if it's in raw form or if it's improved upon, young man. Some gifts are God given. Some gifts are manmade. Then there are some that are cultivated, invested in, refined, optimized, and shared," Terry explained.

"Are you gifted, Luke? And before you answer that, I hope you don't mind me saying that I *know* you're not gifted at selling hot dogs, because I must buy myself into them before you even sell them to me, if you know what I'm saying," Terry chuckled. "After all, it isn't hard to sell a hot dog at a baseball game, but you sure do manage to make it look difficult. So, let me ask you again, Luke, just what *are* you gifted at? And don't say nothing—everyone has at least one gift. Sadly, though, some people never discover what their gifts are. That means that some people never choose to be gifted at anything."

"What are you talking about?" asked Luke, obviously confused.

"For starters, we might have a God-given talent or a skill. We are all gifted. It's part of life, and life is precious. The simple fact that we are born is a miracle. I've learned that firsthand, and because of that, I don't take a moment, or an opportunity, or a gift for granted. For example, my kids are gifts. Life itself is a gift! The fact that we've been given another day is a gift that we shouldn't take for granted. Wouldn't you agree?"

"Uh, I guess so," the vendor hesitantly answered.

"I vow that it is. Let me ask you, Luke, since *life* is a gift, what is it about *our life* that is special? How can we use this gift of life and our unique gifts to stand out, succeed, give, or serve? What puts us in a position to make a difference, to live a life well lived?"

"I don't know," admitted Luke.

"Okay, let me come from another direction. Are you gifted athletically or intellectually? Are you a puzzle solver, a phenomenal marketer, or an awesome artist? Do you have a great voice, are you able to belt out a tune and wow an audience? What is it, Luke? 'Cuz I know it ain't selling hot dogs. I think you're here at the ballpark for a reason, but I'm not sure what it is. There's got to be something that you're gifted at, and if you don't know, I urge you to find out."

"How?"

"For starters, what do people compliment you on, what comes easy to you? The answers to those questions might lead you in the right direction. I'm not messing with you, kid. I *want* you to discover your gifts so you can have a fulfilling life, one where what you do is in integrity with your purpose and your talents."

Then, in a quiet voice, Terry asked, "What are you suffocating behind that hot dog tray, Luke?"

"Maybe I'm not meant to be a major league ballplayer or a rock star. You know, there are lots of average Joes, like me," Luke said.

"I beg to differ. We are all gifted! We all start with the God given ones, but it's up to us for the manmade. Sometimes other people give us gifts; sometimes we choose something to be gifted at. We pursue gifts or invest in practice or experiences to build them. Sadly, there are millions of people who are gifted—they have a photographic memory or can sing like a bird—but they're afraid of the work it takes to make the most of their gift … so they end up selling something they don't believe in for a living. There are people who can figure out how to walk on the moon without a spacesuit, but they're too busy with their Thursday night bowling league to do it."

"And, you don't have to be the best in the world at something, but your God-given gifts are enough to make you good, great, or successful at something! I will tell you that being gifted usually isn't enough. You also have to be coachable and disciplined. You have to study and live a clean life, giving up a cold one with your buddies once in a while. You might have to go the extra mile and risk failure and criticism. You might have to climb the tree of life, but you're afraid you'll get a splinter.

"Tree of life? What's that?" Luke interrupted.

"It's a metaphor I use to describe the rewards in life … the fruits of life if you will, that are worth working for. Things like:

- *"identity"* (how we know ourselves and wish to be known

by others) …

- *"focus"* (where we get to direct our time, talents, and energy and resources) …
- *"peers"* (who we get to spend time with … who we get to enjoy, learn from, or grow with) …
- *"emotions"* (how we get to feel most of the day, most days) …
- *"results"* (measurable accomplishments that ideally serve self and others).

"But you have to do 'risky' things to get these rewards. The enormity of the possibilities and the work required to reach these fruits will cause a lot of people to suffocate, stifle, hide their gifts—shove them aside."

"Luke, I'm going to challenge you here," Terry continued, "I bet you're one of those guys. I might be wrong, but I'm committed to finding out the truth. What is it you can do for yourself or for the game of baseball or the world that you're hiding from us, Luke, because there's a reason you're here … and again, it sure as hell isn't to sell hot dogs. I think selling dogs is out of integrity for a smart young man like yourself."

"How am I supposed to know the answers to those questions?" asked an exasperated Luke. "If I knew what my gifts were, I wouldn't be a subpar hot dog vendor."

"I get it. I get it, Luke. And there's nothing wrong with not being good at selling hot dogs, just as there's nothing wrong with people who *are* good at selling them. Like your friend, Ally, over there. Look at her—she's having a ball! The fans love her, and she looks like she absolutely loves her job. And I'll even go so far to say that I bet she's damn good at it, too," Terry said.

"Yeah, I guess she is. But she's cute, and that helps her get tips, so she has an advantage," Luke pointed out.

"Luke, be fair, is that her only advantage?"

"No, she seems to know everyone … I mean, she doesn't, how could she, but the way she talks to customers is different, like she knows them, can read their minds, finish their sentences, or make anyone laugh at any time. Honestly, sometimes I am not selling hot dogs because I am watching her work. She's amazing."

"She just might be one of those people who could sell snow to an Eskimo—people skills might be her gift. I bet she's never met a stranger. Hey, I have an idea. How about I give both of you a behavioral assessment? What do you think? You in?" Terry asked with enthusiasm.

"What's a behavioral assessment?" asked Luke.

"It's a questionnaire that helps you discover what motivates you and your behavioral style. It's one of the things I do for my clients."

"What do you do?" Luke asked for the second time.

"Yes, you did ask that before, but at the time, I wasn't ready to reveal it. However, I think I can help you. Luke, I'm a world-class coach, speaker, and trainer. In other words, I help people grow, discover their gifts, set their goals and achieve them. If you're willing to do the work and find your gifts, I'll help you discover what they are. But there are conditions …"

"What conditions?"

"You've got to promise to cultivate them and invest in them, instead of hiding and suffocating them. If you can do that, I'll help you discover what they are. I'll help you learn what motivates you and what your behavioral style is," Terry said.

"What's that gonna cost me?"

"It's on me, Luke. Consider it a *gift,*" the older man smiled.

"Why would you do that? I mean, you don't know me …"

"There's plenty of reasons. For starters, it's like fingernails screeching on a blackboard watching you not sell hot dogs," joked Terry before continuing, "also, as many people as there are in the world willing to pay for my help, there are plenty more that I choose to help for free … partly to 'give back,' knowing how gifted I've been, but also strictly afraid of anyone on this planet wasting their gifts—you know, living without purpose. There may be other reasons, but for now I just have this feeling there's something you're not telling me … or willing to admit to yourself. I feel there's something you're hiding from the game, and I have a feeling that the game needs you, Luke. Not necessarily the game of baseball, but definitely the Integrity Game! I have to know why you're here because I'm going to go nuts if I have to watch you fail to sell hot dogs all summer. It's just 20 minutes' worth of questions, so can I gift you and your friend, Ally, a set of assessments. From what I've heard, you really seem to admire her!"

Luke grinned and said, "Okay, fair enough. I'll do it … and, sure, I will ask Ally if she wants to do it, too."

"Good. Here's my card. Send me an email and include Ally's email, and I'll take care of the rest. Now, I'm going to catch the end of the game and see if our rookie pitcher can pull out a win," Terry said as he turned toward his seat. "Before I go though, could you sell me one of your dogs, with lots of mustard?"

"Don't count on that pitcher yet." Luke said as he got Terry his hot dog.

"What are you talking about?" asked Terry as he paid Luke.

"He's only got one good pitch, and he's only using it 18 percent of the time. He's going to have to do better than that to make it in the big leagues," Luke commented.

"Oh? I didn't hear that stat," Terry said.

"That's because they didn't announce it," replied Luke.

"So, you have an inside track to the analytics department?"

"Nah, I might not watch the game, but I can't help but hear the announcers," Luke explained.

"And you pulled a calculator out and did the math?"

"No—just figured it out in my head," Luke admitted.

When the game was over, a curious Terry got online and reviewed the stats. Pulling out his calculator, he crunched the numbers and was surprised at the number that flashed on the screen.

The rookie pitcher threw his fast ball inside 18.3 percent of the time. Maybe Luke's hidden gift has been revealed Terry thought.

4

POTENTIAL

 The next weekend, the Victors were on the road, which made it a good time for Terry to meet with Luke and his coworker, Ally, and conduct their behavioral assessments. He was happy they had emailed him.

When Terry arrived at the coffee shop, the two young adults were already sitting at a table in the back of the room sipping on their iced coffees. Walking up, Terry greeted them.

"I'm glad you both were able to make it today. Hey, Luke, out of uniform, you don't look anything like a hot dog vendor. Maybe we'll be able to figure out what you really should be, or at least, what you're suited for," the season ticket holder said. "Let me get something to drink, and then we'll get started."

Terry kept the mood light during their visit. The last thing he wanted was to have Luke overthink his responses to the assessment—Terry wanted the results to honestly represent the young man's personality. That way, they'd have a true picture of the type of job or career Luke was best suited for.

At the end, the trio discovered that Ally was, indeed, a people person. On top of that, she was already employed in her desired field, food service. And, her assessment lined up with career and life goals, which Terry quickly pointed out.

"See this? This shows us that Ally is in integrity. She knows what her gifts and interests are. She's working in the industry right now and gaining the experience she needs to pursue her goal," he explained.

"What about me?" Luke asked, eagerly leaning forward in his chair.

"Let's see here, Luke. Well, your assessment shows me that you're an analytical person. That's a far cry from being a hot dog salesman. But that doesn't come as a surprise. We both knew that you're no good at slinging franks. Unlike Ally, you're not really a people person. This shows me that you're not likely to be comfortable striking up a conversation with a complete stranger. No wonder you look forward to quitting time; your job is totally out of integrity with your personality."

"Well, according to this, what type of job is best suited for me?" Luke asked.

"It isn't the job that is best suited for you—it's you that needs to be suited to the job. The assessment gives us a list of the types of jobs where you are likely to be successful. But it is up to you to do the work we've already talked about to discover what's important to you—you know, the meaning of your life—and then integrate that with your talents, gifts, and interests. That will lead you to a career that's in integrity with who you are."

"That's the hard part for me," Luke admitted.

"Luke, you've got this. I'll help you—it'll be fun," Ally interjected. "Give it a shot. What have you got to lose, except for a job you don't like?"

"She's right, buddy. We already know some of your gifts. For example, you're phenomenal with numbers and have an amazing ability to crunch them in your head. Who knows, maybe you do belong at the ballpark, but perhaps doing something else, like, say, being in the analytics department or something along those lines," Terry added.

"Nah, what they do is boring. It's the same old stats, all the time, day after day. It's like pitching—everyone throws the same pitches—a slider, sinker, curveball, fastball—but nobody has their *own* pitch anymore. It's all canned," Luke shared.

"What do you think they should do then?" asked Terry.

"I don't know. Maybe actually track some other stuff. Like did you know that your son, TJ, has made two errors since he came to the big leagues?"

"Sure, I follow his stats, Luke," the father remarked.

"What you might not have realized is that 100 percent of his errors are at away games, 100 percent of them were made when *you weren't there*. Does that have anything to do with it? Maybe, but we won't know because nobody looks at that. And then there's our ace pitcher. Did you know that he wins 24 percent more of his starts when his wife is in the stands? And our shortstop has a much higher on-base percentage in day games than night games. Stuff like that," Luke said.

Terry listened, fascinated with the way Luke's mind worked. For the first time, it was the season ticket holder who walked away from their meeting with a lot to think about. The kid definitely had potential, and more than ever, Terry was determined to help Luke tap into it.

***

It was a long road trip, and the Victors weren't on their home field until a week later. Terry continued working with his regular clients though he often seemed to think back to the vendors he'd befriended and wondered if Ally had met up to help Luke yet.

In the Victors' first game back home, the season ticket holder's eyes were glued to home plate when his son, TJ, who earned a spot in the starting lineup during the road trip, faced the pitcher in his first at bat as a starter in front of the home fans. The first pitch was a sinker that nearly fooled him, but he checked his swing in time according to the appeal made to the first-base umpire.

TJ watched the second pitch, a high fastball, go by before fouling off a pitch that came across the outside corner of the plate.

"Come on, son, you've got this," Terry said. "Make him pitch to you."

And TJ did. The next pitch came straight down the pike, and Terry watched as the barrel of the bat gained momentum as it came across the plate, meeting the center of the ball and sending it flying. Terry held his breath as it soared to center field and jumped to his feet as it cleared the fence.

He'd just watched his son hit his very first home run in the majors, and he knew what a milestone it was in both their lives. Terry turned to the aisle when he heard a familiar voice.

"He hit that one good. I almost lost sight of it. Impressive," said Luke.

"Yes, he got a hold of that one!" Terry exclaimed.

"Now he can stop worrying about getting that first one, huh?"

"I guess. It's a milestone that every baseball player looks forward to reaching. But now that he has, I'm sure he'll move onto the next one,"

Terry said.

"What's his next one? His second home run?" asked Luke.

"Perhaps. I'm not sure. I just know that there are milestones in his life."

"If you don't know what they are, how do you know he has them?"

"Because that's how I raised him. I taught him how to fulfill his potential, and he knows what he has to do for his career and for the Victors," Terry advised.

"If I were him, I wouldn't worry about the Victors. The team isn't worried about him—they're only worried about making money," Luke said.

"Then he'd be out of integrity," Terry pointed out.

"Integrity again? Here we go …" Luke rolled his eyes.

"Yes, integrity *again*. You see, if anything is out of integrity, you won't get the results you want. My son's job isn't to be a baseball player; it's to be a member of a team, from the top down. Everyone works together, doing their part to make sure the team reaches its potential, and I'm not just talking about winning games and hitting home runs. The integrity game can be played individually, in teams, or organizations. It's all about making sure the people and the company live up to their potential. But first they have to imagine their potential," the older man explained.

"How do they do that?"

"It's a four-step process. For starters, they have to have a vision. Let's give it a try. Luke, what do you see when you look as far into the future as you can possibly see? I hope you can see farther than hanging out with your buddies tonight," the man said.

"Umm, I don't know. And I wasn't going to hang out with my buddies tonight. Actually, Ally and I are going to get together. Remember she offered to help me find answers to some of those questions you asked me."

"That's good to hear. You know, Hot Dog, I really like her. Now back to my question—what do you see when you look into your future? I get that you don't know that now, but you will, and I think you'll know it sooner than you think. And when you *do* know that, you'll have your vision. Next, what is your mission?"

"What's a mission?" asked the vendor.

"Your mission is the greatest milestone toward that vision. It's a big one, too, even iconic. It's the milestone that proves certain that you really are on your way toward your vision. That milestone for me was when I made my first six-figure income as a coach. When that happened, I knew I was on my way," Terry said.

"And your vision is?"

"To be a world-class coach," the man stated, matter-of-factly. "Vision gets everyone in the stadium, but mission gets everyone seated. And, yes, everyone on the team has a seat—a place and a reason for being there. You have a purpose for being here, to sell hot dogs which we both know you do less than you could. I have a purpose—to support my son and cheer on his team."

"I think I like your purpose better than mine," Luke replied.

"There are some who would love to have your purpose here, especially if it is a step toward their vision, like Ally," Terry said. "But that's neither here nor there. Moving on, we come to objectives. Luke,

I want you to note that a vision is as far as you can possibly see, and a mission is closer, but it's still a way out. Objectives, on the other hand, are even closer than that. They're annual, so they're never more than a year away. They are outcomes. What will the outcome be at the end of this year? How much will you accomplish, and how much closer will you be to your mission and your vision? Then there are goals, and they're even closer. I like to set quarterly goals so I can see my progress toward my objectives. Got that?"

"I guess so," Luke answered.

"What is your objective this year, Hot Dog?"

"I don't have one," the vendor admitted.

"Are you're saying that you see yourself exactly where you are right now a year from now? No changes whatsoever?"

A shrug of the shoulders was Luke's non-committal answer.

"Well, let me get this straight. You don't know your gifts, and you don't have any idea what your potential is or how to get there, so maybe you're right. Nothing will change, and you're stuck slinging hot dogs for the rest of your life," Terry goaded his young friend.

"I don't get it. Why are you riding me so hard?" Luke asked.

"Because I can. Because I see a young man in you who wants to make something of his life but doesn't know how," Terry said.

"How do you know that?"

"Because you're unhappy, and frankly, because you suck at what you do, and it's not a tough job. Selling refreshments at a baseball stadium should be a piece of cake, my friend. I mean, look at Ally over there selling cotton candy. It looks like she's rocking it to me, and she seems to be having a good time doing it."

"I guess you might be right. Selling hot dogs is kind of easy. Maybe that's why I stay here. Maybe I don't want to work hard. I mean, looking into the future sounds like it could take some work, and I'm not so sure I'd be good at it," the vendor admitted.

That gave Terry an idea.

"Maybe it's easier to learn when you teach," he said.

"What do you mean?"

"Maybe if you asked Ally what her vision and mission are, her answers might help you come up with your own. I might be wrong, but I think she probably knows what hers are. Give it a try. If I'm right, you might have your answers. If I'm wrong, once again, I'll buy every hot dog you've got the next time I see you. Ask her if she has a vision. Ask her if she has a mission. Ask if she has objectives for the year. And what goals she's set. You might be surprised with what she shares with you," the season ticket holder said.

"Okay, you're on. I'll give it a shot," Luke agreed.

"I'll do even one better and buy one from you right now. You've been standing here for half an inning and haven't even tried to sell me one, you know," Terry teased as a guilty look came across Luke's face.

"All right—here you go," he said, handing over a hot dog.

"Thank you. Now, here's your assignment, kid. Remember those five fruits we talked about?"

"Yes," nodded Luke, "but remind me what they were again?"

"Identity … Peers … Focus … Results … and Emotions" stated Terry before continuing …

"…What fruits do you see in your life as far into the future as you can possibly envision? Write down what you see … the ways you'll be known … the people you'll be with … to where you'll be directing your resources … the results you will have produced for yourself and others … and what specific feelings or emotions you'll experience daily. Your homework is to visualize those ultimate fruits of life and then ask yourself, what is the greatest thing you can achieve in the near future that would prove you are on your way to that Vision. Then, declare your annual objectives and set quarterly goals that will get you there. If you are willing to do the work, I'm willing to give you feedback," the older man stated.

I don't know. I'm not good with lists," Luke replied, unable to hide his reluctance.

"What you are not good at is selling hot dogs or having the courage to pursue your true potential; saying you aren't good with lists is just an excuse to stay put! Still, if you really believe you aren't good with lists, that's your reality and one of the reasons I suggested working with Ally … perhaps she can do the writing while you are doing the visualizing! Also, think of it as a 'white-board/brainstorm' instead of a 'list'… *the language we use is always integrated with what we believe, while what we believe always determines our behavior* … besides, the only thing you have to lose is a lifetime of selling hot dogs," Terry reminded him in a sarcastic shift from any "heaviness" of his confrontation.

"Okay, okay," the young man laughed.

"Atta boy. Now, I've got to get back to work, so excuse me," Terry said.

"Work? What kind of work? You're at a ball game," Luke laughed.

"Yes, and I have a purpose at this game that is integrated with my potential as a father—to support my son, integrating my gifts of enthusiasm and optimism, while cheering the Victors to a win. Did you catch those three loops for our proverbial shoelaces? Purpose, Gifts, and Potential? Luke, *it's always the perfect time and a ballpark is always the perfect place to be playing the Integrity Game!* And it looks like I've been slacking a bit, so I need to make up for lost time and make some noise," the man said as he turned his full attention to the game and the batter on deck, the all-star first baseman, whose presence was getting a robust round of applause from the stands.

After the game, Luke delivered on his promise when he was talking with Ally. They were turning in their equipment after the game the Victors won easily, 8-2, with help from TJ's bat.

"I was wondering, is this what you want to do for the rest of your life?" Luke asked.

"Actually, no! It's not. Why do you ask, Luke?"

"Well, you're good at it and all, and Terry said you have integrity … that this is the perfect job for you … so I just wondered if it's what you always want to do."

"It is a perfect steppingstone … something I am willing to do now on the way to what I really want to do. Don't get me wrong, I like working here, Luke. I love the crowds, for sure. And I really know the game after countless hours at a ballpark growing up, when I was watching my brother play. And I really like food service … you know, the snack bar in my brother's Little League was 'world famous' so they would always say … and where else do you want to be when you have to watch your brother play baseball for three hours? The snack bar! When I really didn't want to be at my brother's game, getting to go to the snack bar made me happy. I remember knowing my dad didn't want to be interrupted while he was coaching or announcing games, so I could always get money from him to go to the snack bar. I went from buying candy once every two innings when I was six to getting paid to work evening shifts when I was 16. When I was 10, we even experimented with deep-frying Girl Scout cookies for a special dessert … it didn't work with Thin Mints because the chocolate melted, but Samoa's deep-fried in pancake batter with a splash of chocolate sauce and bathed in whip cream was my favorite creation, and it was a HIT with kids *and* parents… that is, until the other Girl Scout Moms found out and protested that it wasn't fair that only one girl got to provide the snack bar with all the cookies. Then I had to let my whole troop supply them, and it cut into my personal sales by seven 8ths…I had 100% of the idea, but only got 1/8th of the sales! Then, other troops petitioned the Little League to be able to sell, and it got political and ultimately nobody was able to sell at the snack bar," Ally "remembered out loud" with an 'ah, those were the good old days' smile on her face!

Now, Ally was clearly a bit enamored with and lost in her memories as she continued, "I was always number one in Girl Scout Cookies sales in my troop because my parents and I would get creative about how to sell them … and most of the time, I had to stop or share my ideas because of complaints from other kids or parents that weren't as creative or risk-taking. 'It's not fair,' they would say. 'Life's not always fair, and losers never think it is' my dad would say and then he would ask me if I wanted to be average or above average."

"All my friends in my troop wanted to sell with me when my dad would drive us up to the University on Saturday mornings to knock on college students' doors, instead of competing in our neighborhood where everyone had a daughter or niece in Girl Scouts already. I also remember going to Toastmaster's meetings with my dad, giving impromptu and persuasive speeches to sell cookies to his fellow Toastmaster's ... yeah, when I was like nine. He once even got his Business Club to do a 'Cookies and Cocktails' event where there were special adult beverages that were paired with the different flavored cookies ... we always had so much fun ... 'work hard, play hard' Dad would always say.

An amused and tranquil look came across Ally's face as she almost crossed that threshold of reminiscing that had her talking out loud to herself, seemingly forgetting Luke.

"Maybe it all started then, now that I think about it," she concluded literally as if to herself.

"What started?" asked a super attentive and "drawn-in" Luke, who was hoping to re-establish a connection with Ally he felt had been interrupted by the clear recall of her childhood memories.

To Luke's relief, it worked and snapping her back to the present, Ally continued ...

"Well, if you want to know the truth, what I really want to do—what I guess I have always wanted to do—is to own my own food truck where I make all the rules and decisions free of the restrictions or limitations or mediocrities that I observed growing up. Very few things make people happier than eating, and I know I am here to use my creativity to make other people feel happy ... joyful! So, I really want my own 'world famous snack bar' but mobile with the freedom to serve many parks instead of just one. Then, I'd like to have a whole fleet of them and ultimately my own food service that caters to baseball crowds of all sizes, from the Little Leagues to the Bigs!" she said with excitement.

"Wow! So, your vision is to have your own fleet of fan-friendly food trucks?" Luke said with a smile that was met mutually by Ally from the alliteration of the 3 F's … fan-friendly-food.

Luke, encouraged both by Ally's smile and what he was beginning to see in his own mind, went further …

"That would mean that your mission might be to get your first truck, I guess …" Then, almost as if to himself, but still out loud, he continued, "and your objectives this year could be building your resume, getting licenses and permits, or even designing a branding strategy!" Luke exclaimed in a bit of disbelief at how clearly he was starting to see the four stages of Ally's Potential!

Now it was Ally's turn to bring Luke back to a present mindedness, "I love how you are thinking," she said encouragingly, "*Totally*, I am on a mission to get my first truck. My objectives are a little different than what you imagined, but I have them … and then I set my 30, 60 or 90-day goals based on my objectives. I break it all down … kind of how you just did!"

"So you already know about Vision, Mission, Objectives, and Goals?" Luke asked, in a combination of suspicion and let down, hoping he'd have something to teach … hoping he'd be of value.

All of a sudden, he was too nervous to ask what was going through his head, which was a gnawing question: *You didn't happen to learn from the season ticket holder who did our assessments did you?* Luke instead spent the next 15 minutes telling her what he, himself, had learned from Terry about potential and the four-stage process toward declaring it.

When Luke was done, there seemed to be something mutually understood but as of yet unspoken between Luke and Ally ... instead of sharing where she had learned about "potential," she asked if Luke was ready to imagine and declare his!

And just like that, another Integrity Game had begun.

5

GOAL SETTING

Luke and Ally and arrived at the ballpark early for the next game. "Hey, Luke," Ally beckoned, "I'm going to run to the upper deck to get an autograph and one of the free bobbleheads they're giving out before they're all gone. Do you want to come with me?"

"Sure, I'll go. But I don't necessarily need a bobblehead, or an autograph, for that matter. I didn't know you were into that kind of stuff," he replied.

"Oh, yeah. Like I said, I've spent a lot of time at ballparks, and I've learned to love the game. I've even set a goal to get the autograph of every player on this team. Today, they're featuring TJ, and I think it would be cool to get a bobblehead in his likeness," she explained.

"Every player? You have an autograph for every single player on the team?"

"I sure do. I try to get it right away, in case they get traded or are sent down to Triple A on a temporary basis when a starter is injured on a rehab assignment or something. Oh, and I even have autographs from the coaches and the general manager!"

"Really? Well, okay, I'll tag along. We've got time before the game starts," he agreed.

That day, two players were being featured in the giveaway, TJ, the rookie, and the right fielder for the Victors, a Gold Glove winner who is a fan favorite. The two men sat side by side at a table with their own bobblehead in front of them. When Luke and Ally arrived, it was still very early and there were only about a dozen people in line, waiting patiently for their free souvenir and what they hoped would one day be a valuable autograph.

When it was her turn, Ally first approached the right fielder, handing him a piece of paper to autograph. Then, she stepped to the other side of the table where TJ sat, not far from where Luke spotted Terry, coincidentally standing nearby.

"Hey, Luke," Ally said, "will you do me a favor and get a picture of me and TJ?"

Thrusting her phone into his hand, she ran around the table and kneeled down by the ballplayer. Tossing her arm around his shoulder, she held up his bobblehead next to his face and gave a big grin while Luke flashed their photograph.

Then, she really surprised her coworker by giving the rookie a hug and saying, "See ya later!"

Not knowing what to think, TJ froze momentarily before saying anything.

"Do you know him?" Luke asked. "Are you really going to be seeing him later?"

"What are you talking about? Oh, that—it was just a figure of speech, kind of like 'see you around.' I didn't mean anything by it," she explained.

"Oh, I just wondered, considering you gave the guy a hug and all."

"It was nothing. I'm just glad he was a good sport and let me get a picture with him!"

As they were walking away, Terry approached them.

"Hi, you two. Beautiful day for a ball game, isn't it? Ally, I see you got my son's bobblehead. Maybe it'll be worth something one day," the older man said.

"I got his autograph, too," she giggled, showing him the piece of paper.

"Yeah," Luke interjected. "Ally just told me that it's her goal to get the autograph of every single Victor player."

"Who is your favorite?" Terry asked Ally.

"The last autograph is usually my favorite, so right now, I'd say it's TJ," she replied, smiling, knowing Terry would like that comment about his son.

"You sure you don't have a crush on him?" Luke asked, trying to keep any hint of jealousy out of his voice.

"On TJ? Oh, no! He just seems to be a cool guy, that's all," she said.

"Luke, I notice you didn't get a bobblehead. I take it you don't have a goal to get souvenirs and autographs like your friend, Ally, here," Terry pointed out.

"No, I'm not into all that stuff," the vendor replied. "I'm having a hard time believing that Ally has a goal to get *all* of them!"

"It's a respectable goal, and we know that it's just one of her long-term goals. Now that you brought it up, how are you doing on living your own purpose and creating your own goals?" asked Terry.

"Well, I have been thinking about it, but I haven't gotten very far. I haven't set any goals, that's for sure. Maybe I'll just see what pans out and go from there," Luke answered.

"From experience, I can tell you that most people fail to set goals, so the good news is you are not alone!" Terry said with a chuckle, then continued, "… the bad news is that you probably don't know *why* most people fail to set goals … and the funny newsflash is that if you knew why you were failing, you would have this new dilemma of either doing something about it or knowingly choosing to continue to fail!"

"Okaaaaayyyyy!" Luke playfully dragged the word out in a voice of surrender. "You got my attention again … why do people fail to set goals?"

"Batter UP!" Terry exclaimed as he playfully received the permission to continue, "Luke, there are five reasons—all very easy to understand—and your job will be to figure out which of the five are *your* barriers and then work through them. We can't beat the enemy until we identify the enemy… and a huge enemy of success is failure to set goals!"

"Only five reasons?" Luke confirmed.

"Yes, and in no particular order of importance, the first one I'll share is that a lot of people avoid setting goals because they don't know what a goal really is…they mistake it for a hope, a wish, or a dream. Ambiguity of language lets us get away with that. Like people believe they are setting 'resolutions' every year in January, but are they truly 'resolute' if statistics show that most resolutions are abandoned before February 1st? It is my experience that people abandon resolutions because the behavior they are modifying is never attached to a goal. It's one thing to say you will go to the gym five times a week and another to say by April 1ˢᵗ you will be able to lift 22% more weight than you can today. One is a behavior; the other is the GOAL of the behavior. At any rate, a goal is the 'integration' of two things: the 'what' that is to be achieved and the 'by when' it is to be achieved. It's that simple."

"Okay, so make sure I have a 'what' and a 'by when' in my goal … or if there is not 'what by when' it isn't a goal, yeah?" Luke confirmed with a simplicity that showed Terry really did have Luke's attention, but also showing Terry that Luke might have explained it even better *because* of the simplicity.

"Yes!" Terry said in an excited and grateful tone, almost a relief that Luke was dialed in and getting it. Terry continued, "And, the second reason they fail to set goals is because they don't know the importance of setting goals, and I think that might be an issue with you. Goals are fueled by the power of visualization," Terry explained.

"What's that?"

"Have you ever heard of the law of attraction or what is called reticular activation? Here's how it works—once we tell our mind what we want, our mind will look for ways to get it. It's pretty cool, like deciding you want a yellow Vette, and suddenly you start seeing yellow Vettes everywhere you go," the season ticket holder said. "The mind is focusing on what you want and actually helping you make it a reality. The brain is incredible at pattern recognition, but without telling it exactly what we want, it is far less sure what to look for and recognize. Again, it's the power of visualization, and I'll bet you that every one of those ballplayers on that field have been taught to 'see the success they desire in their minds' as part of their practice and training regimen… or how the military developed virtual reality technology for training battle simulation that people now play for fun in their homes. Setting goals is one thing, *seeing* them is another!"

"That is cool!" Luke exclaimed. "So, goals are important because they program our brain to know what to look for—and I guess what to avoid, as well, so we stay on track, like punching the address in to someplace you've never been on MapQuest … you tell it the destination and it helps you see all the 'how to'? Am I getting it? What else is there?"

"Getting it?" Terry interjected, "Luke, twice now you have said it better than I did! You're batting two for two with three more swings! Another reason people fail to set goals is that they're afraid of failure. Plain and simple. Their ego doesn't want them to fail or risk embarrassment, so the goal-setting process gets sabotaged somehow, usually by the vagary of 'hopes, wishes, and dreams' that are missing the accountability of 'what by when'" said Terry.

"I get that. Nobody wants to admit that they failed, for sure, so please don't remind me again how much I suck at selling hot dogs today, okay?" Luke said playfully before thoughtfully continuing. "That one hits home for some reason. I mean, I just got done saying I'll let things play out and see what happens… like fooling myself into believing I'll be successful whatever comes my way, instead of deciding what I want in order to shape 'the way'…my goodness, what a difference!?"

"YES!" Terry almost couldn't contain himself, but quickly settled down. "And on the other hand, another reason people fail is a reason most people wouldn't expect—they're afraid of success," Terry stated, encouraged by the depth of Luke's listening.

"No way!" Luke exclaimed.

"Oh, yes, fear of success is very real. If you told your buddies you were going to do something great or difficult, they might not believe you. They might take you down and punch holes in your aspirations because they are afraid that you'll change and abandon them ... worse yet, your effort will reflect their laziness. Peer pressure isn't just about doing something bad—often, peer pressure is about preventing you from doing something great! They don't want you to change, and you might be afraid of how you'll change, or be evidence that they are underachieving, and you don't want the drama, so you accept the status quo," Terry said.

"Okay, that makes sense, too, like a couple weeks ago when the extra inning game was a chance to make more money, and I was complaining that I had plans with my friends." Luke said.

"It can be worse than that, Luke!" Ally interjected in a 'no longer able to contain herself' tone, "My brother almost wasted a college scholarship because he was afraid to outgrow his family, afraid to outgrow his friends, afraid of the work it would take to learn a new city or adapt to a new environment. He had a full ride, he worked hard and deserved it, and almost wasted it," Ally quickly added, and just as quickly Terry interrupted nervously...

"I believe you're *both* getting it," Terry emphasized with a 'silencing' tone and 'don't interrupt me' glance that seemed out of character for him. "But be clear," he continued, "goal setting will still be difficult because the fourth reason people fail to set goals is that they do not know how. I think you are ready to learn how."

"I already know how," Ally interrupted with a playful smirk, "my *parents* taught me," she added even more playfully as if she was telling a joke that only she understood, " …you two carry on. Luke, I'll see you at break time, I am going to put my bobblehead away in the employee locker room before our shift starts," Ally said while peeling away from their goal-setting stadium walk-n-talk.

"She's amazing!" Luke exclaimed. "It feels like I know her, like really well, and then she does something or says something, and it feels like I'll never know her—and all that does is make me really want to know her … like what is going on in that brain of hers? She's cute and all, really cute, but she makes me think and she makes me want to be smarter."

"Hey, Romeo, can we finish up on goal setting? I mean, what am I? Chopped liver? I am trying to get you to think and be smarter, too, and you'll need to be if you really have a goal of deserving a girl like that!" Terry revealed.

"Sorry about that, I mean, she's young enough to be your daughter, but even you would have to admit she is distracting!" Luke said with a "boys club" wink that wasn't mirrored the way he'd hoped, which restored Luke's focus. "And these reasons for not setting goals make a lot of sense. So far, I'm guilty of all four—you're a genius!"

"I can't take total credit because I learned those reasons from one of my mentors, Brian Tracy," the man revealed, giving credit where credit was due.

"But there is another reason people fail to set goals, and I discovered this on my own. It's because when they set goals, they are making a commitment to pain. We know that most human beings automatically seek to avoid pain. It's about the evolutionary hard wiring of surviving of self-preservation. But I believe there are two kinds of pain. There is pain of growth, which is sacrifice, will power, and hard work. For instance, when your friends are partying and you're studying—it hurts when you have to sacrifice or feel like you are missing out or 'suck it up' to get through one more chapter of notes or a test or quiz. It hurts, but that pain leads to good grades, confidence, opportunity, etc. Growing pains!

"The other type is the pain of regret. It's when you know what you are capable of, but you aren't doing anything about it. Then you grow old, and life goes by and you find you're not happy. Underachievers and unsuccessful people believe they can avoid regretting the past by never setting goals in the first place ... very similar to fear of failure but different because it isn't the result people are afraid of NOT getting—it is the WORK people are afraid of DOING, result or no result. Because they don't want to embrace growing pains, they never set goals. But I am here to tell you that a directionless life in itself is painful," Terry said, "and it's certainly no way to deserve a girl like Ally!" Terry concluded with the "boys club" wink Luke had searched for earlier.

"So, I get that you're saying that I need to set goals, but how am I supposed to know what kind of goals to set?" Luke asked.

"Good question, Hot Dog. Basically, it's identifying what you want in your life to be different. There are four forms of different, and that's something I call CICR. Ask yourself what in your life needs to be different. Where are you willing to do something different in order to get different results? What hurts? What would feel good if you could make it happen?"

"That doesn't sound too tough. What does CICR stand for, though?" Luke asked.

"Change, Improve, Create, and Remove. It's a process. Let's go over each, one at a time:

"Change—what is in your life that is not going away that doesn't look the way it should? Your finances? Your relationships? Your career? Whatever it is, you need to change it. From what I know of you already, the need to be employed is not going away in your life but selling hot dogs might need to.

"Improve—what is going good? What is in your life that IS working, 'Give me more of that, please!' What do you want more of? Those are areas of your life to increase and improve. From what I know of you already, you have more to give to baseball and you probably want to improve your relationship with Ally, yeah?" Terry surmised before continuing.

"Create—what doesn't exist right now, but you have to create it? For most people, it is something like goals, understanding our gifts, finding our purpose, resources, strategies, even beliefs and stuff like that. From what I know of you already, you have more success education in your life than you did before we met.

"And here's the last one, Luke. Remove—when I say remove, I'm referring to the toxic stuff. It might be negative people who are holding you back or bad habits. Whatever it is, if you want to grow, you have to get rid of it. I don't know your friends, I don't know your parents or if you even have parents, I don't know if you have siblings or other co-workers who show up 180 degrees from how you see Ally, but the first thing I ever learned about you was you believed baseball was 'just a game' and it was okay to cheer against the home team in front of its fans, and that hanging out with your buddies on Friday night was more important than making the money you were complaining you weren't making enough of. With my help, I believe you have removed some of that 'stinking thinking' and you might have to remove some more to set your goals!"

Luke's jaw dropped as he realized, as if being struck by lightning, that it was true. He simply wasn't thinking in those ways anymore … now he was eager to hear what Terry had to share and looking forward to beating the enemies of goal setting to get closer to deserving a girl like Ally. Lots of things were all beginning to integrate in obvious vs. subtle ways.

"Do you think you can do that, Luke? Ask those questions, and ask yourself what the greatest thing is that you need to achieve in the next three months?" Terry asked.

"I really think I can. You have given me a lot to think about, but I really think it'll help," Luke agreed.

"Good, now before you set those goals, I want to make sure you set goals that will spur success," Terry commented.

"How do I do that?"

"By setting SMAART goals. Make them specific. Don't say you want to make more tips—state the exact dollar amount. Make sure your goals are measurable, so you know what progress you've made. Make them achievable—don't set goals that are impossible or improbable to achieve, and NEVER set a goal that you do not believe you CAN achieve. Ambitious—is the second A … it isn't about the size of the goal, but more so what behaviors you have to decrease, increase, start or STOP in order to achieve the goal, like the resolutions I mentioned earlier, except sticking to them until the goal is achieved! Then there's the R, which I say stands for Reward. What's your why? The bigger your why, the bigger the reward, and the more you'll be willing to do to make it happen," Terry explained.

"Right now, it's easy to use 'deserving Ally' as the motivation, but please let me encourage you to have more than one reason. *If you have one reason for wanting something, you might get around to working on it, but if you have SIX reasons for wanting something you can be UNSTOPPABLE!*"

"Unstoppable ... I never thought of myself that way. Okay, what about the T?" asked Luke.

"A necessary ingredient, for sure. The T stands for Time. It is the "by when" that you will achieve the "what." A goal has to have a date attached to it. Otherwise, it's a hope a wish or a dream like we said a minute ago ... uh, okay, 12 minutes ago," Terry said, laughing at himself for being so long-winded as he is often described by those that know him best.

By then, they had returned to their stadium level and section as Terry was ready to take his seat.

"Don't let all my hot air fool you. Just focus on the 'what' you want and the 'by when' you want it. I recommend looking three months out. Finally, they don't have to be perfect…focus on the word "draft," just draft some goals. If you do that, I can take a look and help you get them SMAART. It's like I am standing at the hurdle ... you run, you jump, and I help you get over if needed, but no one is going to push, pull, drag, lift, or throw you over the hurdles in life. You have to run and jump. Most successful people in life are willing to help the ones willing to run and jump!" he concluded.

"Thanks, Mr. uh, Ter, uh, Dad?" Luke joked, after stammering, not knowing how to address Terry, who was teaching him life lessons like a parent would.

"If you are committed to doing the work and getting the help, call me Coach Terry for now … we'll work on 'Dad' or just Terry down the road, okay?" the season ticket holder shot back, playfully integrating the humor with the serious. Moving forward, in this Integrity Game, his 'player piece' was Coach Terry!

6

STRATEGIES, TACTICS, AND RESOURCES

Every great coach or manager has a strategy for winning, whether it's matching the right pitcher to a batter, making defensive changes, or even something as broad as an overall strategy to bring in fresh, young players by trading proven players who are near the end of their prime.

Of course, the Victors had a strategy, and throughout the season, it was being executed well. Their goal was to play October ball, and if it weren't for injuries to a few key players after the All-Star break, they would have made it as a wild card team. But, as the season entered its last month, the team and its fans were already focusing on next year.

Terry felt melancholy set in as the number of games dwindled down. He knew he'd miss the ballpark atmosphere that he'd cherished for so many years, but this year, the feeling would be even more pronounced, given that his son was now in the big leagues.

Yet, in another way, Terry looked forward to the off-season because it gave him an opportunity to put more of his focus into helping others enjoy an integrity-filled life. That was the thought that crossed his mind at the end of the Victors' series against the Legends, a matchup that always ensured a sold-out stadium. The standing room only status spilled over into the concourse, which Terry had entered at the end of the game.

As he so often did, the season ticket holder spotted Luke and Ally as they wrapped up their shifts. The fact that the young hot dog vendor was standing idly while his fellow coworkers were obviously busy with tasks piqued Terry's curiosity enough that he took a few steps closer.

Just at that moment, it appeared that Luke's supervisor also took note of his lack of activity.

"Hey, Luke, don't just stand there. You've got to finish inventory and fill out your reports," the woman said.

"I already did," Luke replied, matter-of-factly.

"C'mon, you just checked back in five minutes ago. There's no way you could have completed your end-of-shift reports," she said.

Without a word, Luke retrieved his paperwork from the bin behind the counter and handed it to her.

"Here you go. I think you'll find that it's all here," he said.

After seeing that the forms were completed in their entirety, his supervisor asked, "How did you manage to get this done in such a short time? It takes half an hour—that is, if you do it right."

"If you do it the long way," Luke responded. "There is a faster way, though, and trust me, my numbers are right."

Speechless for a moment, his supervisor stared at the forms, then turned to the young vendor and said, this time in a non-assertive tone, "Can you show me how you came up with these figures so quickly?"

Terry watched intently as Luke went through the forms line by line. Unable to hear what was said, he could, however, tell that the supervisor was no longer doubtful. In fact, if his observations were right, and they usually were, she appeared to be quite impressed.

Keen to hear what had just taken place, the season ticket holder stuck around, hoping for a moment with the young man.

"Hey," Luke said when he turned around and saw Terry standing across the walkway. "Every time I turn around, it seems like you're watching me."

"The word is observing, Luke. It's what I do, and I'm quite good at it," Terry smiled. "Can I ask what just happened there? I couldn't help but overhear part of the conversation, and I'm intrigued. After all, it seems like you've been done for some time, and your friend, Ally, and other coworkers are still hard at it."

"I know," Luke smiled, seemingly proud. "It's nothing really. I just figured out that there is a faster way to come up with the sales and inventory figures than the steps they're making everyone go through. Seems my boss is interested in having me share it with everyone so they can start using it next season."

"Oh? That's interesting. I'd be interested in hearing it, too. Does that mean you'll be coming back next season?"

"Yeah, I guess. That is, unless something else comes along, but I doubt that'll happen," Luke stated.

"I think the off-season will give you an excellent opportunity to do some self-discovery—you know, to play the integrity game and figure out what your goals and talents are," the coach remarked.

"I agree, but it would be better if I already had some idea … but I don't."

"If I may make a suggestion, I think it would help you to walk through the process, even if you don't have the answers yet."

"How can I do that?" Luke asked.

"Well, how about helping Ally? After all, she *does* know what she wants, and I think she needs to begin the process of making that happen. Now, according to the assessments you both took, I think there are areas where Ally could use your help. Besides, correct me if I'm wrong, but I'm thinking you might enjoy an excuse to spend some more time with her," Terry said with a knowing smile.

"It shows?" Luke asked a bit sarcastically, admitting the obvious.

"Let's just say I'm a keen observer and we'll leave it at that, okay, Hot Dog?" Terry grinned as if to suggest Luke wasn't *too* pathetic with his obvious crush on Ally.

"Okay, but how can I help Ally? She seems to have it all together and she knows what she wants," Luke pointed out.

"Oh, yes, she's got a lot going for her, but her personality type usually lacks some of the organizational and analytical skills necessary. That's where you come in. I've noticed several times that you're talented in that area, and you just reinforced my belief with your supervisor," Terry said.

"But I don't know where to start. I'm not sure how I can help Ally," Luke said.

"I have an idea. Why don't you stop by my office next week and talk about it?" the older man offered.

In that meeting the following week, Terry explained three critical areas Ally would need in order to start a successful food truck business.

"Strategy, tactics, and resources," he said. "Ally knows what she wants, and the next step is determine how she's going to get there. A business plan is a set of strategies, and I'm guessing that Ally has one, or at least a portion of one already. That business plan should have strategies for marketing, finance, manufacturing, and distribution. There's even an exit strategy."

"Okay, I get that. But I still don't see how I can help," Luke admitted.

"You will. You see, every strategy needs a tactic," Terry explained.

"What's that?"

"Tactics are observable actions and behaviors that execute the strategy. If there is a five-point strategy, there will be five tactics to execute it," Terry shared. "Then there are resources, which help you execute the tactics. For example, a tactic might be to get funding, so a pitch deck could be created as a resource to make that happen."

"Okay, I'm following. So, you think I might be able to help with tactics? Or resources? Or both?"

"I think you can help in all three areas, because you and Ally are not alike. There are things that I'm sure she can do exceptionally well, but her personality type is typically not great with the details, analysis, and pesky stuff like licenses and regulations. However, your assessment showed that those are likely among your strengths. Do you get where I'm going?" asked the season ticket holder.

"I think so, but I don't know anything about business plans and stuff, so ..."

"That's where I come in. I'm going to walk you through what you need to know right now. Let's start with strategy. It's not difficult because like the wheel, strategies are already out there for anyone to access. Tony Robbins says success leaves clues. Everyone who has been successful has had a strategy, and it's nothing new.

"Now, let's break it down a bit. Strategies fall into a few major categories: Sales, marketing, operations, and finance. You need to have a plan for each area."

"Why? I mean, can't you just wing it?" Luke asked.

"Good question, and the answer is no. You need a plan. What if Ally needs money to run and grow her business—who is going to give her money unless they know what it's going to be used for, when they'll get it back, and what they'll get in return? Another reason she needs a plan is to shape or guide the choices and behaviors of employees and vendors. This goes back to why the business exists in the first place. Imagine an employee who encounters a situation that they don't know how to respond to. They can turn to the business plan, which provides the mission statement and that will help them identify the options that will guide their decisions and behaviors, so they integrate with the company culture.

"The third reason is for succession planning and exit strategy. If someone is an entry-level employee, how do they get to the top? And here's something a lot of people don't think about—what happens to the business when the owner decides to retire or move on. Are they going to sell it? Let it die? Give it to their kids or perhaps their employees? These are things that should be decided *before* the business opens, not after."

"Okay, I get that. Is there anything else?" Luke asked.

"Yes, and it's a big one. Every business owner needs a plan because they have to know if the business is worth having or running. A lot of people have a dream they are passionate about. They say it's something they really want to do, but that's nothing more than code for 'I don't want to look for a job and be micromanaged by someone I don't respect.' Sound familiar? People think they have a business, but they have an income-earning hobby at best. Usually, there is no accountability. It's one reason why I play the integrity game—these people are out of integrity."

"Ah, integrity again," Luke smiled. "It sure is your game."

"You bet it is. You can't have integrity if you aren't accountable. And that's where you come in, Luke. I want you to walk Ally through the 12 accountabilities she'll need to be successful. I call them the Terry 12 Step," informed the coach.

Teaching Luke the 12-step process took a few meetings as the season was concluding, but Terry wanted to make sure the vendor was well informed. Not only did he want the young man to know the process, but he truly thought that by helping Ally through it, it would benefit both of them. Perhaps, giving Luke a reason to tap into his gifts and talents would be the nudge that would point the vendor in the right direction.

***

Between his meetings with Coach Terry, Luke was the topic of talk among some unlikely people at Victor Stadium. His supervisor was so impressed with his streamlined inventory and sales reporting process that she brought it to the attention of the team overseeing vendors and sales at the stadium.

On one unseasonably warm day in the beginning of September, vendors were scrambling to restock ice and cold beverages. As he prepared for the game, Luke heard other vendors yelling back and forth. "I need more ice! Keep the ice coming! Make sure you have plenty of beer in those coolers! We're going to need it today!"

After 15 minutes of voicing the need for ice cold beer, Luke spoke up.

"As hot as it is out there, you ought to be putting more effort into getting some of that water on ice. You're probably going to triple your water sales today. On scorchers like today, beer sales fall about 30 percent. It's just not refreshing at these temperatures" he remarked.

"Hey, you worry about your hot dogs, and I'll worry about the beer," the middle-aged man said.

Shrugging his shoulders, Luke walked away, only to be stopped by his supervisor.

"Hey, Luke, are your stats right?" she asked.

"That's what it's been in the past. Heck, before this game is over, you'll probably hear them yelling because there's no cold water," he remarked.

And that's exactly what happened. While her crew was out selling food to the fans, she got to witness Luke's prediction play out in real time.

"I hate to say I told you so, but he told you so," she said to the man managing the booth next to theirs.

"Who? That kid? What does he know?" the man snapped.

"Apparently something you don't," she replied, suddenly proud of Luke. *He might not be the greatest hot dog salesman, she thought, but I'm glad he's on my team.*

On another day, an order was placed by the analytics department, and in those cases, vendors typically delivered the orders to the staff. On this particular occasion, his supervisor turned to find her closest employee, which was Luke.

"Here you go, and don't be too long. I need you out there in the seats," she said, handing him the order.

The analytics team was friendly, and they were known to tip well, so when they made small talk, Luke was happy to oblige.

"Thanks for bringing it to us. We're starving but too busy to leave our station," one remarked.

"No problem. It's my job," Luke replied at the same time that another member of the team asked if anyone had a rookie stat he needed.

Without thinking, Luke spoke up.

"His batting average was .288 when they brought him up from Triple A," Luke said.

"Thanks," the guy said, turning toward his computer monitor. "Wait a minute … who are you?"

"I'm Luke. Sorry, I'm just delivering your hot dogs. I didn't mean to butt in," he replied.

"You knew that off the top of your head?" another man asked.

"Uh, yeah, I guess so," Luke responded.

His reply set off an avalanche of questions, testing Luke's memory and knowledge. To everyone's surprise, including Luke's, he knew the answers to eight out of the 10 questions. Then, excusing himself, he returned back to the stands, where he did his normal mediocre job of selling food at Victor Stadium.

When his shift was over, his supervisor pulled him aside.

"Luke, I got a call from the manager of the analytics team. He wants you to give him a call. Here's the number," she said.

When Luke returned the call, he was surprised to be met with the manager's praise, saying that his team was impressed with his ability to recite player stats—so impressed, in fact, that they wanted to offer him a part-time position in the off-season. If he was interested, they could use a hand with end-of-season stats and getting their records up to date in preparation for the next year.

7

TERRY'S 12-STEP PROCESS

When he wasn't working with the analytics team, Luke kept busy helping Ally with her business plan. Following Terry's instructions, Luke explained to her the different strategies she needed in her business plan and worked with her to create tactics to execute each strategy.

Most of their time was spent going through the 12 accountability steps that her food truck business would need to be successful. He'd spent a great deal of time studying them beforehand, so he could communicate them to her in the right way.

"Ally, I think you've got the first step, which is to deserve the customers and their sales. The way Terry explained it to me, you have to believe in your stuff and what you offer. It's about passion for what you do, too. I think this one is easy. I mean, what's a day at the ballpark without food. Everyone wants it, loves it, and needs it," he explained.

"This next one, though, might be something to work on. Step two of Terry's 12 step is to be a Chief Operating Officer. Terry showed me that running a business is different than doing what you're passionate about. You love food and making people happy, but there's a lot more to running a business, so this one is going to take some thought, don't you think?"

"Yes. After all, I've never run a business before. Maybe Terry can explain what that entails," Ally replied. "So, what's the next one, Luke?"

"Again, it's one that I think you've got a good handle on. Products and services. What are you selling? What are people willing to give you in exchange for their money? How does it differ from the competition? I know you have recipes and innovate offerings in your head, but I think we'll need to figure out what you're really going to offer to start."

"I can do that! It's already in my head, but I can put it in writing and make it part of my plan," she said, jotting a note to herself.

"Great. Moving on, we have info in, info out," he remarked.

"What does that mean?"

"It's about market research. Here's what Terry said. Bring info from the marketplace into the company so the company can make good decisions about the information it puts out into the marketplace. It's about market research and market penetration," Luke explained.

"What? Market research? Oh, Luke, I'm doomed. I hate research, and I don't even *have a clue* where to start," Ally wailed. "What am I gonna do?"

"Calm down, Ally. I can help you. Thankfully, this is one area that I've found that I am kind of good at. I actually like numbers, percentages, and stuff like that. Why don't you let me take responsibility for Step #4? I'll do the research and figure out your competition, customer demographics, and regulatory climate," he offered.

"Thank you so much, Luke! You're so smart, and I need your help, that's for sure. I don't even know what regulatory climate means!" she exclaimed.

"Well, you don't have to. I think your time and effort would be better focusing on what you are good at," Luke remarked, sharing a comment Terry had told him.

"Cooking?" she smiled.

"Eventually, but for now, you have other things to think about, like a logo, a slogan, T-shirts, stuff like that," he said.

"Oh good, that's something I *can* do. It'll be fun," she grinned. Ready to move on, she asked what was next.

"Sales, in particular, converting them. This is another step that you're already awesome at, Ally."

"Thank you," she smiled broadly.

"But like Terry said, it could be a problem. You're probably the best salesperson I know, but at some point, you're going to have to run the business, so you'll have to train others to do what you do so well. So, it looks like we'll need to create a training program for your employees," Luke stated. "Whether they're selling food or you need someone who can get approval from park districts before you can bring your truck to their games, you'll have to have a team and teach them what to do and how you want it done."

"Wow, there's a lot more to this than I thought there would be. I wonder if I'll ever be able to do it all," she sighed.

"You will. Like Terry told me, you need to have strategies, tactics, and resources. Once you have those, you have a plan for success," Luke assured her, proud of the fact that he'd paid attention when

Terry explained the purpose behind his 12-step process.

"Here's another one that I think you're already good at—customer service. You do a great job at customer service, so your customers come back and they refer other people. I think you've got this one, Ally," Luke commented.

"The eighth step is operations or facilities management," Luke advised.

"Is the food truck the facility?" she asked.

"Yes, but it's also about where your food truck is. Is there electricity, running water? What do your customers have access to, and does it improve their experience or not? Another part of this is knowing who to turn to if something needs attention or something is broken. That could be different people for different purposes.

"Moving on, the last four steps Coach Terry taught me are in Finance. Accounts payable is making sure the lights stay on and the phones are working. Businesses have expenses and must arrange for the paying of those expenses in a way that protects cash-flow and good credit. Accounts receivable is all the different ways a business collects revenue and there are many strategies for effectively receiving revenue. One quick tip to guide you is this: *Make it as easy as possible for people to pay you … in all that you do, make it easy to pay you!*

The 11th accountability is transactional finance. It's about accounting, bookkeeping tasks. Super simple. Knowing line item by line item how much is coming in and going out. Reconciling all the numbers and preparing for tax reporting."

"Again, that's another area where I struggle … math and numbers are so boring to me, Luke, but numbers are your thing—I could really need your help here!" Ally admitted.

"Maybe you'll need an accountant," he laughed. "Anyway, there's only one step left so let's get to it. It's strategic finance."

"What's that?" she moaned.

"It involves how much money you want to dedicate to strategy— setting budgets and making strategic decisions about money ... like whether you want to pay your employees a commission and, if so, how much ... or how much you want to dedicate to researching and developing what you will be selling ... or how much money you are willing to invest in marketing. It could be that you want to commit a percentage of sales toward expanding your business and purchasing a second food truck," he explained.

"So, it sounds like strategic finance is making decisions about what will happen to the money, whereas transactional finance is documenting what actually happens to the money," Ally summarized before continuing, "and I don't think I want to be in charge of either of those jobs!" she concluded with playful laughter.

"Well, let's chart it out then" Luke assertively suggested.

Knowing what they needed to do, they returned to the first step and made a chart, assigning different steps to each of the areas of accountability, making sure they utilized each of their strengths to ensure that Ally's food truck business would have every chance to be successful.

"So, what now, Luke?" Ally asked.

"Now we type this up, and we get to work and create a plan. From there, Ally, I'd say you'd have the information in your hand to take the first step in making your dream happen," he said.

"Which is?"

"Getting the money you need to purchase your first food truck," he grinned.

"Oh, I hope so. I've wanted this for so long, Luke!"

"I know you have. Let's work together to get this ball rolling, and when we get it done, I say let's have Terry take a look at it. He seems to have a lot of contacts. If we play our cards right, he just might help us," Luke said out loud.

"Oh, I know he will!" Ally agreed.

"You do? How do you *know* that?" Luke asked, skeptically.

"Uh, well, I don't really *know* for sure," she quickly retorted. "But he does seem like such a great guy, doesn't he? And he really seems to want to help you, so I guess I thought he'd want to help me, too."

"I think he is a great guy ... I guess I just didn't realize that you knew him as well as I do. But you are the people person," Luke remarked.

"Yes, I am," Ally replied with an easy grin. "Now, come on, we've put in a long day. I think we deserve a break, don't you?" she asked, grabbing his hand. "What do you say we go mix a little business with pleasure and check out our competition—I'd love an ice cream cone right about now!"

8

INTEGRATING WORD AND COMMITMENT WITH ACTIONS AND BEHAVIOR

 "Let's see what we have here," Terry said, looking at the copy of the plan that Ally and Luke proudly handed to him as they entered his office.

"Hmm, I do want to say I'm impressed. It looks like you spent some time on this. Sit down while I look more closely," Terry said as he gestured toward the two comfortable chairs in front of his oak desk.

"So, do you really think it's good?" Ally asked with anticipation.

"I haven't read it all, but it's a good start. I can say that," the older man admitted. "Luke, it really looks like you kept the 12-step process in mind when you two created this plan. I am interested in reading about your strategies to make it happen."

"We can rewrite them if you don't like them," Luke quickly volunteered.

"No need for that just yet. Keep in mind, too, that there can be more than one possible strategy for accomplishing something. That doesn't mean that one is right, and one is wrong. It simply means that you have a lot of choices when it comes to strategies. There are multiple paths to a single destination, something that's called equifinality. I know that sounds complicated, but it's really quite simple. Basically, the best strategy for you might not be the best one for me," Terry remarked.

"Why?" Luke asked.

"Because the best strategy is one that is matched to your behavioral style. Luke, you're analytical, and Ally is social. She's a people person, so it's only logical that you would have different strategies, but they would all have the same goal in mind. And they can both accomplish their purpose," Terry said.

"Now in looking over what you've created here, I'm also looking to see what each of you have committed to. Then, I determine whether those commitments are really strategic. I think you'll agree that we can all do a hundred things in a day, but they're not all integrated with what you've committed to do. But look at it this way—even if you've committed to do several things in a day, how many are you actually going to complete? I want to help you look at those things and decide if you're really going to do them or if they're going to stay on the list and carry over to tomorrow, then next week, and so on."

"We'll do them!" Ally assured him.

"That very well might be the case. I do want to caution you, though, that when it's time to be your word and do what you'll say you're going to do, you have to be realistic. And you have to be honest with yourself and with the people you've committed to. Sure, we all fall short from time to time, but I'm not here to find places where I think you'll fail. I'm just pointing out that there can be an opportunity here to look at places where improvements can be made."

"I think we're being realistic, and I also believe we are committed to what we said we will do on that paper, Terry," Luke said.

"I'm sure you are committed, but I also know that it's easier to say we're going to do something than it is to follow through and actually do it. As a coach, it's my job to make sure you live up to that … and just as important, to keep you in communication if you find it necessary to break your word for whatever reason," Terry responded. "Face it, sometimes things happen, and we can't do what we said we'd do. I get that, but it is the communication and follow-up part that I want to reinforce. If you can't do what you say you'll do, step up and reach out and let the other person know what's going on."

"Well, when we committed to doing the things we put in that plan, we had very good intentions. We didn't just say we'd do it, so we had something to write down," Ally said.

"Oh, I'm sure. And that brings up a good point. What I want the two of you to know is that people tend to judge themselves based on their intentions, but others judge them according to their actions. That's like comparing apples and oranges; they are two entirely different things," Terry explained.

"Hey, I thought we did a really good job there. We thought it out and made a plan. Now, I feel like you're looking for something wrong," Luke said defensively.

"Whoa, I'm not looking for anything wrong. This isn't an attack against either of you. As a matter of fact, I'm looking to see what's right. I don't want either of you to make a commitment you can't keep. And I don't want anyone to have cause to feel disappointed with the other. Rather than having to deal with that later, let's take a realistic look at what you both say you're going to do. If it sounds feasible, then we can set up a plan to be accountable, either getting it done when you say you will or being accountable by providing an update to each other when you can't honor your commitment when you said you would. Deal?" Terry asked.

"Deal," Luke and Ally answered, simultaneously.

"Words are powerful, but behavior is so important, especially in relationships. That's why it's important to manage expectations. Doing what you say you'll do when you're going to do it is evidence of integrity. When I talk to clients, I ask them, 'Are you your word? What is your relationship with your word?' You see, your word when kept builds trust, and once trust is gone, it's difficult to get it back. But if you can't meet your original commitment, you can still maintain that trust, that integrity, by communicating and bringing your word current. It's as simple as saying that something came up and you won't be able to complete your task by Friday, but you will have it done by Monday. It's not always about doing what you'll say you'll do—it's more about staying in contact and updating your word when you need to."

"Okay, I think I get it," Luke said.

"The next point I want to make is that people often commit to doing things that aren't really strategic. By that, I mean that they're keeping busy and taking action all day long, but those things aren't part of their strategy. John Wooden, a famous basketball coach, once said, 'Don't mistake activity for achievement.' I can't say it any better than that. Staying busy might be good, but is that busyness getting them where they want to go? Busy doesn't always mean progress," Terry said.

"Well, do you think our commitments are strategic?" Ally asked.

"Let me see," Terry replied, glancing through the papers before him. "Oh, here's one. It says here Ally that you'll experiment with at least three recipes a day so you can decide what your food truck will offer. While that is something you do have to determine, it might also be busy work that makes you feel like you're getting something done," Terry said.

"I do have to know what to sell!" Ally answered.

"Yes, you do. And the actions you take do have to support your word and commitment. Actually, that's the next thing I wanted to focus on, your actions and behaviors. Can you see how those two things would integrate with our word and commitments?"

"Doesn't it mean that it's not just what we *say* we'll do, but what we actually do? Oh, and our behaviors, wouldn't that be our habits, like if we tend to procrastinate and put things off until later? Stuff like that?" Luke replied.

"You're on the right track, Luke," Terry said. "Behaviors could also be about being indecisive. Think about it, if you're indecisive, you might not be able to make a decision. Of course, that would impact you. Behaviors are what you actually do—when others are watching, and even more important, when you don't know anyone is watching at all.

"Every day, people make decisions on what they're going to do that day, and this plan outlines what you're both committing to do. What actions will you take? What will your behaviors be, and will they be different when you don't think anyone is paying attention? These things do matter. They signify your integrity," Terry said.

Going over the plan, Terry pointed out several areas where Ally committed to do something, and the coach questioned her.

"Ally, are you sure you said you'd do this because you *want* to do it? Or are you simply agreeing to anything for the sake of being agreeable? That is one of your behavioral traits, after all. My concern is that you're committing to things that don't interest you at all," Terry mentioned.

"Like what?" she asked.

"Let's see," Terry said, looking the document over. "Here it says that you'll create a survey to determine what foods to sell. Now, we both know that data and statistics aren't your thing. Is it realistic that you'll actually do this and complete it when you said you will?"

With that remark, Ally became defensive.

"That's not fair, Da--!" she snapped, before stopping abruptly. Sighing, she started over. "Darn it! What I meant to say was that I *can* crunch numbers."

"Wait a minute," Luke interjected, coming to Ally's defense. "How do you know that's not her thing? Can you figure that out from a single behavioral assessment?"

"I didn't mean to offend anyone," Terry explained. "And to answer your question, Ally is a people person. Her behavioral style usually doesn't do well with analytics. I was just pointing out an area where activity might be confused with achievement."

Realizing that the two had perceived his comments as an attack, Terry made an effort to redirect the conversation. From there, the trio spent the next 20 minutes going over the rest of Ally's plan. While he was realistic and pointed out aspects of the plan he thought needed addressing, he also found that he was, indeed, impressed with other parts of the plan, and he was sure to comment on them.

"Luke, I am particularly impressed with the parts of the plan that discuss permits, licenses, and health requirements. You seem to have a good grasp on the paperwork and permissions Ally will need in order to begin. Actually, I'm surprised you knew about those things," the coach admitted.

"I guess I learned about that stuff from my dad," said Luke.

"Oh? Was he in the food service industry?" asked Terry.

"Actually, he was a vendor. He was a vendor with a business housed in Victor Stadium," the young man advised.

"Really? What does he do now?" Terry asked. "Is he retired?"

"No," Luke answered hesitantly. "Actually, he passed away when I was 13."

"Oh, Luke, I'm so sorry. I didn't know," Ally said, warmly reaching out to touch his arm.

"I'm sorry to hear that, as well. What happened, if I'm not intruding?" Terry asked.

"He had a sudden heart attack. It was unexpected. There weren't any signs or anything. They said there was nothing they could do," Luke explained.

"Again, I'm sorry. So, is that why you decided to work at Victor Stadium? Remember, I told you there was a reason you were there. Is it because of your dad?" asked Terry.

"At first, it wasn't. When I was a kid, I wasn't fond of the ballpark," admitted Luke.

"Why not?" Ally asked.

"Well, as we both know, the schedule isn't great. So, while other dads were home on weekends and nights, mine wasn't. While most fathers were taking their kids to the ballpark to watch games and make memories, the only time I went to the stadium with my dad was when there was nobody else to watch me that day. You and TJ were probably out there having a great father-son day, rooting for your team and buying souvenirs, while I was wiping counters, getting buckets of ice, stocking napkins and plates and refilling ketchup and mustard containers," Luke complained.

"If you didn't enjoy your time at the stadium, Luke, why did you decide to work there?" Terry asked with genuine concern.

"Well, when Dad died, the management told my mom that when I was ready, I'd always have a job there if I wanted one. So, when the time came, I took them up on the offer," Luke explained.

"But you don't like selling hot dogs," Terry pointed out. "So, I still don't understand why you accepted the job."

"In hindsight, I guess I hoped that being at the stadium would make me feel close to my dad. Who knows, maybe I hoped that working there was something that would have made him proud," Luke said, shrugging his shoulders.

"Did you get what you hoped for?" Terry asked softly.

"No. I don't feel close to my dad when I'm there. And I think it's a stretch to think he'd be proud of me. After all, it's no secret that I'm just a mediocre hot dog vendor," Luke reminded Terry, giving him a small knowing smile. "But it hasn't been all bad. After all, I got to meet Ally … and you, of course, Terry."

"But I'm not your dad," Terry softly finished the thought that was in Luke's mind.

"No, you're not," Luke agreed.

"Well, while I'm not your dad, Luke, I do think your dad would be very proud of you. I know I am," the season ticket holder said with an increased sense of admiration for the young man he was getting to know and growing to like.

9

LEARN AND GROW

 "Ally, we have to tell him. It's time."

"But what if he gets mad? What if he hates us?" Ally cried.

"We can only hope that he'll hear us out and give us another chance. I think he's a reasonable person. He'll come around. But like I said, we can't do this anymore. It's not fair to him."

"Can't we wait a little longer? Give me some time; I'll try to think of something ..." she pled, thinking of excuses.

"No. There's nothing to think of ... nothing to say. We're past that point. I know you don't like it, and it won't be easy. But we got ourselves into this situation, and now we have to face the consequences. It's time to tell him the truth."

"But it's not like we *lied* to him," Ally argued.

"It's not like we were totally honest, either. He's going to find out sooner or later, and I think it'll be better if he hears it from us. The longer we keep silent, the harder it will be—for all of us."

The next time they met, Terry opted for a different environment. He expected their meeting to be short and thought perhaps it would be an opportunity to be casual, so he sent them a text asking them to meet him at Romitos, a quaint Italian restaurant not far from Victor Stadium. It was a popular neighborhood restaurant that was well known for their realistic Italian atmosphere and their authentic pizza.

***

Luke walked in the door and looked around, noting the wide planked wood floors and the red and white checked tablecloths resting under candleholders made from wine bottles dipped in wax. Even though it was highly frequented during the baseball season, the neighborhood regulars preferred to dine there during the off-season, when the atmosphere was quiet and more intimate.

Looking around, Luke spotted Terry and Ally sitting at a table in the back of the room.

"I'm not late, am I?" Luke asked when he approached the table.

"Oh, no. You're right on time. We just got here," Terry said. "As a matter of fact, I walked in right behind Ally, and we just sat down."

"Good," Luke said, sliding in the booth beside Ally. "So, what's on the schedule today?"

"I'm glad you asked. Actually, I just wanted to follow up on our last meeting, which was about words and commitments, as well as actions and behavior. Today, we're going to talk about learning and growing because it comes on the heels of those other principles," Terry shared.

"Sounds good. The pizza smells so good, and I'm starving—so let's get started!" urged Luke.

"Your word is my command," the season ticket holder laughed. "No, seriously, learning and growing comes from experience. I think you'll agree with that. But today I want to talk about another way we learn and grow, which is through mistakes."

"Everybody makes mistakes," Ally pointed out.

"Yeah, but nobody wants to make them," Luke added.

"Those statements are both true. However, I think Luke pointed out something that I want to touch upon, which is nobody wants to make mistakes," Terry interjected. "That's because society has labeled them as bad things. In my opinion, that's an incorrect stigma, and it probably came from the mindset that we learn from trial and *error*. Nobody would argue that errors can be bad. We see them in baseball, and we see how they have a negative impact on the results of a certain play or the entire game, right?"

"Right," Luke nodded.

"The word mistake conjures fear. We relate it to blame, fault, or shame. If we allow that façade to keep us from being willing to make mistakes, we aren't going to grow and learn. I think that mistakes can be a good thing … think about them as learning disguised by discomfort or inconvenience. Learning is the essence of growth, and growth is the essence of achievement. So why don't we refer to the process as 'trial and learning,' or even 'trial and growth,' and get rid of the negative connotation?"

Without waiting for a response, Terry continued.

"What I want both of you to take away from this conversation is that mistakes can be a good thing. They can teach you a lot in a short amount of time. And when you learn from them, you'll avoid repeating the mistake again. And that's where they're beneficial. You see, you absolutely will make mistakes, some big, some small. It's your job to use what you learn from that mistake to improve. So, make mistakes! Make as many mistakes as you can so you can get better and better!"

"So, you're saying that mistakes can be a good thing," Ally replied.

"Well, they do have a return on investment," Terry agreed.

"A what?" Luke asked, unsure if he'd heard his mentor correctly.

"A return on investment. I call it a Mistake ROI," Terry shared. "You see, I learned long ago that nobody is immune or exempt from making a mistake. They are going to happen. It's not the fact that they happen that is an issue. Oh, no. I learned that when I make a mistake, my response to it will determine the outcome."

"Here, let me show you how it works," Terry said. Turning a paper placemat over, he created a small chart.

MISTAKE R.O.I.

M (Mistake)	C (Consequence)	L (Learning)	R (Reward_

From there, Terry demonstrated how to fill out the chart, using a fictional mistake.

"Let's say I burned my hand because I touched a hot iron after my parents told me not to. So, the mistake is touching the iron, right? Going to Column C, what are the consequences or costs of that? One was pain! Another was that my parents had to pay for a doctor visit. And then my parents yelled at me, and I got in trouble for not listening to them. Learning is the next column. What did I learn from this? Oh, I learned that it hurts to touch hot things. I learned to listen to my parents. Now, let's move on to the last column, which is Reward. This is where the ROI comes in. The reward is what you gained from making that mistake," explained Terry.

"What are the rewards of getting burned?" Luke asked.

"Well, for one thing, I learned not to touch hot things, so I haven't been burned since. And how about the fact that I haven't had to spend money on medical bills from getting burned since that time. And then I can also say that my relationship with my parents improved because they knew I'd learned my lesson and, next time, I'd probably listen to them the first time. Basically, the rewards state I learned and grew from my mistake. Do you follow me?" asked Terry.

"Yes. So, Ally, we need to make sure neither of us get burned in the food truck," Luke teased.

"In the beginning, that might very well be a concern," Terry agreed. "But mistakes can happen to the most seasoned entrepreneurs. I recently was reminded of that."

"You? You make mistakes? But aren't you Mr. Integrity? What mistake did you make?" Luke asked, still in a playful tone.

"That is my expertise, but like I said, mistakes happen to all of us. It doesn't matter if we're a rookie or a veteran," Terry said. Then clearing his throat, he continued.

"Luke, do you remember the last time we talked and you mentioned that you took your job at Victor Stadium because of your dad?"

"Oh, no," Ally softly muttered, before placing her hand on Luke's arm. "Luke, let me say that I am sooo sorry."

Luke looked at Ally and could see the pain in her eyes. Confused, he looked across the table at Terry and said, "What's going on here?"

"Let me finish. I asked you if you'd found that bond with your dad at the stadium, and you said no ... but you had met Ally, and me," Terry said.

"Yeah, and then you said that you weren't my dad," Luke replayed the scenario, still waiting to hear where this was going.

"That's right, Luke. I'm not your dad. But there is something I haven't told you. Luke, I am Ally's dad," Terry informed him.

"What? No, your *TJ's* dad," Luke corrected him.

"Yes, and I'm Ally's father, too," the mentor calmly added.

"Wait ... I don't get it ... What the ...? Why didn't you tell me? Why the big secret?" Luke thought out loud, his voice becoming a bit more agitated with each thought.

"I'm so sorry," Ally repeated, this time with tears in her eyes. "Please don't hate me," she pled.

"Luke, I want to apologize. Perhaps it was a mistake not to tell you, but I do want you to know that we had good intentions. You see, Ally talked about you all the time, telling me how much fun she had at work with you and how you always volunteered to help her restock and complete her reports, and you made sure you walked her out to her car after every game. But she knew that you didn't like your job, and she wanted you to be happy. She told me how much potential you have, and she truly wanted to help you. Seeing how much it meant to her, I agreed. But as I grew to know and like you, I knew it was out of integrity for us to keep our relationship from you. Please accept our apologies and know we meant well," Terry explained, then waited for a response.

"I don't get why you lied to me!" exclaimed Luke.

"I acknowledge that it might have been a mistake for us to withhold that information, but let's be honest, Luke ... if I had told you, would you have been receptive to my coaching or would you have steered clear of me?" asked Terry.

That remark hit home, and Luke didn't quite know how to respond. In frustration and disbelief, he felt like he needed space and time to think.

"I don't know what to think—I gotta go," he said, moving Ally's hand off his arm.

"No, don't," Ally's voice broke.

"It's okay," Terry nodded. "I understand. Just know that we have learned from our mistake. And we'll both be there for you when and if you're ready."

As Luke walked out the door, Terry tried to calm his daughter down.

"He needs to let it all soak in. Just give him some space. I think he'll come around," Terry assured her.

Ten minutes later, their pizza was delivered. Ally's father placed a slice on her plate, but she refused to touch it.

"Come on, Ally, at least taste it," her father urged. "Starving yourself isn't going to bring him back."

"You never know—it might."

They quickly turned their heads to see Luke standing next to the table.

"Mind if I sit down?" he asked.

"Of course! Grab a plate!" Terry encouraged him. "Can I ask what brought you back? Was it only the pizza?"

"No. I thought about how much Ally means to me, and I didn't want to throw that away. And after I thought about it for a few minutes, I believe your intentions might have been good, But there's another reason," Luke stated.

"What's that?" Terry asked.

"I really want to know what kind of ROI you got from keeping your big secret," Luke stated.

"Hmm, well, I've learned that full disclosure is the best policy," Terry answered. "I'm now reintegrated, and my words align with my actions. And I trust that this 'mistake' will pave the way for us to improve our relationship, Luke. Oh, and there's one more thing— now, we can actually ask you to join us for the holidays," Terry smiled.

"Oh, Luke, do you forgive me? I'd love for you to have Thanksgiving dinner with us," a still upset Ally said hopefully, while a single tear escaped her eye and fell down her cheek.

Seeing that she needed reassurance, Luke put an arm around her shoulders and, without even thinking, gave her a gentle kiss.

Looking up, he saw Terry and remembered that he was Ally's father, not just a random baseball fan.

"Oops, I'm sorry, sir. That might have been inappropriate, given that you're Ally's dad and all," Luke spoke with sincerity before he shifted his tone and jokingly added, "But in my defense, I had the best of intentions."

10

ACHIEVEMENTS

Luke and Ally spent the next two months in a whirlwind of activity. Luke was putting his newfound analytics skills to use at Victor Stadium, and along the way, he was asked to create social media posts to encourage engagement and interaction prior to the next season. As it turned out, the young vendor found that he had another gift—conveying messages that piqued interest through the written word. This came as a surprise to those who knew Luke as someone who didn't like to attract attention, but Luke found that he really enjoyed working behind the scenes, or the keyboard, that is.

When he wasn't earning a paycheck working for the team, Luke devoted most of his time to helping Ally with her food truck. And things were moving along faster than either of them had anticipated, thanks in a great part to Terry's involvement. Ally's father had put feelers out to people in his circle, letting them know his daughter was in the market for a used food truck—one that could be customized if need be. The main concern was that it needed to be equipped and in good operating condition. In the beginning, at least, there wouldn't be a large budget for renovations.

It was a loan officer who let him know about a client who was preparing for retirement and wanting to sell the food truck he'd operated for the last several years. A couple inspections and more than a few negotiations later, Ally was the proud owner of her first food truck, paid in part by her father, who became her first investor, and in part by the banker who reviewed their business plan and approved a loan to cover the rest.

In a routine meeting with Luke and Ally to discuss their progress, Terry asked them what they had achieved.

"Well, I have a food truck, and that's huge!" Ally eagerly announced. "And Luke and I have done tons of research, too."

"What have you learned?" Terry asked.

"For one thing, I know what kind of food people want when they go to a ballgame. I know what kind of oil is best and the best temperature to deep fry food in," Ally replied.

"And you, Luke, what have you got?" Terry asked.

"Well, sir, I've read just about every single health department code at least half a dozen times. I can recite every permit and license Ally needs in order to open her business. I know exactly what utilities her food truck will need, and ..." he paused, pulling out papers from the binder in front of him, "we've figured out who the customers are that we'll cater to."

It was evident to Terry that they were proud of the work they'd done, which was why he hated to burst their bubble. But he knew he would be doing them a disservice if he didn't speak up.

"I can see that you've learned a lot, and that's a good thing. But let me ask once again, what have you *achieved?*"

"We just told you, Dad," Ally reiterated.

"No, you didn't. You told me what you learned. Sure, buying the food truck was an achievement, but have you actually prepared any food in it yet, Ally? You can read and review recipes from dawn to dusk, but that doesn't make you a master chef. And you, Luke, you can recite every requirement, code, and agency that you need to get approved, but have you approached the park district, township, or a league at all?" Terry posed.

"Uh, no, but ..." Luke began.

"What I'm trying to get at here is that there is a difference between education and experience. You can learn and learn ... and no doubt, you have ... but you also need experience. Here is how I teach this to my clients: *Experience plus knowledge equals wisdom. You have knowledge, but until you take action and gain experience, you won't have wisdom,*" Terry stated. "And there is always—always—wealth in the wisdom."

"And before we go any further, I want to clarify something—I'm not just talking about a little experience, say cooking a batch of hot dogs. No, I'm talking about *accumulating* experiences. Nobody goes to a gym once and walks out with a six pack, right?" Terry grinned. "Of course, they don't. To get those kinds of results, they have to go to the gym and work out a lot—they have to accumulate actions."

"Let me get this straight," Luke interjected. "You're saying that in order to get really good, we need to do things over and over, right?"

"Kind of. You see, you can't be the best, an expert, at anything if you never do it. Ally can't have the best food truck in town if she hasn't served anyone. Luke, knowing what to do isn't going to get the gears rolling for the licenses you need. I'm saying you've been educated, and education is knowledge, but training is experience. In education, you learn things, but in training you *do* things. Here's an analogy — would you hire a surgeon who sat in a classroom or lecture hall and learned what to do in surgery, but who had never performed a surgery before?"

"No way!" Luke replied.

"No, you'd ask them how many surgeries they'd performed, and how many successfully, wouldn't you? Because those would be among the surgeon's achievements," Terry explained.

"It's like I told TJ, you can study a pitcher's pitches and the films over and over and over, but until you step up to the plate, stare him down, and actually figure out how to hit the ball, *consistently,* you can't say you've got that pitcher's number ... come to think of it, baseball is an excellent analogy for this principle, because baseball keeps thorough records of a player's achievements. You know that, don't you, Luke?" Terry asked.

"I sure do. And in the food truck business, would achievements be number of burgers or hot dogs sold, stuff like that?" Luke asked.

"Sure, that counts. Achievements are getting behind the scenes stuff done, like permits and licenses. When you're open, achievements might be being the most popular vendor or food truck. Selling the most burgers is an achievement. How about being the most requested food truck? The fastest service? A fan favorite?" Terry replied, throwing out possible achievements.

"So, let's start over. Luke and Ally, what are your achievements? Do you have any at all? Are they positive achievements or negative achievements? Getting locked up in jail eight times in eight years, for example, is an achievement, but not one that is integrated with growth," said Terry.

"There's that integrity word again," Luke smiled.

"Yes, funny how integrity ties into just about everything we talk about, isn't it?" Terry agreed. "Now, let's sit down and see if we can actually start chalking up some of those achievements, because the way I see it, if you get the ball rolling quickly, I think opening day might apply to more than baseball this year," Terry smiled.

"Really? Oh my gosh, in that case, I have soooo much to do!" said Ally. "I mean, I don't even have a name for my food truck yet!"

"Wait a minute, Ally. I think your dad might be onto something—did you hear what he just said?" Luke remarked.

"Yeah, opening day—we have a lot to do …" Ally replied.

"No, before that … fan favorite. How about Fan Favorite Foods? Or…"

"Wait—you're close! How about Fan Friendly Food! I love it!" she exclaimed, reaching out to give Luke a hug.

There was a lot of work to do, and they somehow got it done. Terry suggested that they create a checklist of all the achievements that would be necessary before they opened for business. Luke and Ally eagerly set out to create it, and when they were done, it looked daunting. But Terry assured them that it was all possible, and the key was to make sure everything was integrated with their purpose, their word and commitment, and their actions and behaviors. Their achievements would be the proof that they were acting in integrity, as each step played a role in supporting the overall outcome.

Every time they met, Terry opened with one question: What are your achievements? And before the off-season was over, the Fan Friendly Food team proudly handed over a list of the achievements they'd accumulated.

- Gained an investor
- Obtained a loan
- Bought a food truck
- Named the business!
- Designed a logo
- Designed T-shirts
- Created a menu
- Created a social media page for the business
- Obtained suppliers
- Passed health department inspection
- Obtained local and state licenses
- Received approval by park district to operate during Little League tournaments
- Signed contract with Commissioner of Park Board
- Interviewed and hired four employees
- Gained official endorsements by TJ and the Victors

Ally and Luke eagerly waited for Terry's reaction as he reviewed the checklist.

"Well, Dad, what do you think?" Ally asked, holding her breath for his reply.

"Well, kids, I have to say I'm proud of you. It looks like you've built yourselves a good foundation—one where you've each integrated your strengths and gifts. So, when do you open?" Terry inquired. "On opening day?"

"No, we actually open before that, Dad," Ally giggled.

"Oh?"

"Yes," Luke said. "With TJ's endorsement and our connections with the vendors at the stadium, we're going on the road, Terry, and officially opening Fan Friendly Foods during a spring training exhibition game!"

"Really?" Terry couldn't hide the surprise in his voice. "Now, that's quite an achievement!"

11

GIVE—SERVE

It was a beautiful spring day when the Fan Friendly Food truck pulled into the ballpark at the Victors Spring Training Facility in Scottsdale, Arizona. Excited and anxious, Ally turned to Luke and asked if he had seen her dad and TJ for the umpteenth time.

While this was Ally and Luke's "grand opening," it was also a special day for Ally's brother. Historically, the first exhibition game during spring training was a fundraiser, and this year, it supported the Miracle League, a nonprofit that enables kids with disabilities to achieve their dream of participating in the Great American Pastime.

The Victors had already announced that TJ would be in this season's starting lineup. Despite not even having a full season under his belt, TJ finished in the top 10 vote-getters for the Rookie of the Year Award. Already a fan favorite, the Victors looked for opportunities to put TJ in the public eye, and there was no occasion more fitting than this first game in the preseason.

And for good reason …

TJ had grown up playing baseball with his best friend, Nate. They played catch in the backyard and fielded for each other during hitting practices. But unlike TJ, Nate never had the opportunity to play organized sports. Born with a slight disability that left him with muscle weakness in one leg, Nate was just like any other boy their age—except for the fact that while TJ and his friends were at practice, Nate, or as TJ called him, "Bubba," was at physical therapy.

As a blessing in disguise, it was through Bubba's challenges that he made his mark on the world.

Today, the inseparable duo would reunite for a worthwhile cause.

"Hey, Ally, I think I see TJ," Luke commented. "And your dad's there, too, talking to some guy. I'm going to run over and let them know we're here."

As he approached the table where TJ sat, Luke heard a child exclaim, "Wow! Look, that's TJ, number 48, autographing ballcaps! Let's go get one!"

As kids swarmed around the table, Luke walked up to Terry and his companion.

"Hi, there, Luke," Terry said. "There's someone I want you to meet. This is TJ's good friend, Bubba. We go way back."

After making small talk for a few minutes, Luke excused himself. "I better get back to Ally. She's put a lot of pressure on herself and needs all the help she can get today."

"You two will do just fine. You prepared for this. Maybe she just needs a little pep talk from her father," Terry remarked.

"It couldn't hurt," Luke agreed. "She's been asking where you are for the last hour."

Fifteen minutes later, Terry had calmed Ally down, reminding her that today was also her shining moment, and no matter what, she had every reason to be proud. After all, this was her dream and her passion. She'd learned everything she needed to know and had trained her staff well. No matter what, she was ready for the experience.

"Hey, they're walking onto the field," Terry pointed out.

It was TJ who stood on the mound, while the rest of his team lined up behind him. But instead of holding a baseball, TJ was holding a microphone. As the spokesperson for the Victors, he had been asked to open the ceremony before the first pitch of the fundraising game.

"Welcome to spring training and the Victors' annual fundraiser for the Miracle League," TJ announced. "I became familiar with the Miracle League through my good friend. Many of you know him as Dr. Nate, but I've always called him Bubba. Bubba and I grew up together. We did everything together—we rode our bikes and played catch. Basically, we were inseparable everywhere, except on the baseball field. You see, Bubba had a physical disability that prevented him from playing baseball, but that didn't stop him from being there for just about all of my games. Outside of my father, I'm pretty sure Bubba has been my biggest fan since my first Little League game.

"Nate might have been *my* biggest fan, but what he doesn't know is that *he* is my hero. You see, I know I'm fortunate to be able to play in the majors, but my friend has done something even bigger than me. He has overcome his challenges and used them to make sure that kids with disabilities have the opportunity to do the things he couldn't do. Today, he's Dr. Nate, a physical therapist who works with children to overcome their challenges and disabilities. He reminds us that it is through our challenges that we can find our passion and purpose. And he has done that through his work with the Miracle League, where he is committed to making sure that the dream of playing baseball can come true for every child.

"In order to help people like Nate continue their mission, all proceeds from today's game are being donated to purchase much-needed equipment for the Miracle League. In addition, we'd like to invite our fans to welcome the addition of the Fan Friendly Food truck to this year's event. Stop by and enjoy some fantastic ballpark-quality food, and the Fan Friendly Food team will also donate a portion of their sales to the Miracle League," TJ concluded.

"Now, it is my pleasure to ask my friend, Dr. Nate, to join me on the mound and throw the ceremonial first pitch in today's game," TJ said, before he had the opportunity to watch his friend, Bubba, receive a standing ovation as he took the mound in a professional sports game for the first time.

Off to the side, there wasn't a dry eye as Terry, Luke, and Ally listened to TJ's heartfelt speech. When he trusted his voice, Luke said, "Wow, Bubba is an amazing guy!"

"He is," Terry observed. "And so is TJ. And while we're at it, I'm pretty proud of you and Ally, too. You're all following your own path, one that uses your talents and passions, one that is leading you to your purpose and, ultimately, a life of integrity. Bubba is proof that it is all integrated—our gifts, purpose, passions, words, actions, and behaviors. They provide us with amazing achievements, one of the biggest of which is to give back and serve others, which is what all of you are doing today. Just look at what Nate and TJ have accomplished. And now, look at how far you and Ally have come and the experience you are beginning to embark on."

"Unbelievable, isn't it?" Luke replied, placing an arm across Ally's shoulders and holding her tight.

"I think it is quite believable, Luke," Terry said. "Like baseball, life is a game of integrity. When you play with integrity, son, you put yourself in a league where you can knock your dreams out of the park."

It was a touching moment, and Luke had to clear his throat before responding.

"Because of you and the integrity game, I've come a long way in the last year," Luke said. "How can I thank you for everything you've done for me?"

"That's easy. The last principle in the integrity game is giving and serving. We got a firsthand glimpse of it today and the impact it has on everyone around us," Terry encouraged before lightening the conversation a bit.

"And speaking of serving, Hot Dog, do you think you can try to actually sell a few hot dogs this year? Given what I'm seeing, it might not be too difficult," Terry laughed, as he pointed to their food truck, where the line was quickly growing.

"I'm ready," Luke replied. "Come on, Ally, it's go time!"

As he watched Ally and Luke running hand in hand toward their new adventure, the season ticket holder realized that while his children's dreams were coming true, so, too, were some of his.

Everything was integrated … just as it should be.

12

AFTERWORD:
LETTER FROM THE AUTHOR

Dear Reader:

Thank you so much for the time you invested in reading The Integrity Game®. You have helped, and hopefully continue to help, me put *The Integrity Game®* out into the world as *a comprehensive approach to personal and professional growth*!

Now that you've seen Luke's journey, let me attempt to help you apply this in your own life, team, career, family, or business.

First, recall how Luke experienced each "point of integration" on the model starting in Chapter 2? Recall how Luke succeeded or struggled to answer the sets of questions Terry asked from chapter to chapter thereafter?

Next, remember how Terry tied Luke's shoelaces into integrity in Chapter 2? For The Integrity Game® keynote speeches and workshops I deliver, I created a slide that uses the shoelace metaphor to depict the ten points of integration. Can you see how the graphic on the next page illustrates my 10-point model and previews the 10 "question sets" that I believe we all want to answer in order to improve our integrity? Can you see, the journey that Terry took Luke on in Chapters 2 through11 (starting with Purpose and ending with

Service)?

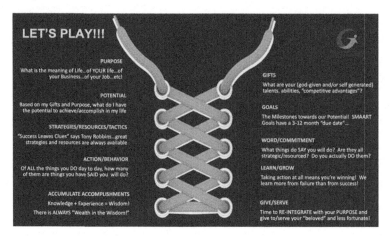

Recall that Luke struggled with these questions ... as if they were somehow unfair to even be asked, but not so badly that he refused to play the game! Also recall that, for himself, Luke never really answered ALL of the questions Terry asked of him.

I say that because, at first, you may not be able to, either. And you certainly might not be able to without a Terry (external accountability source) who is willing to ask the tough questions ... who cares about you (or the boy his daughter likes) enough to confront you! *Left to our own devices, we excuse ourselves more often than we confront ourselves!*

So, will you allow me to ask YOU questions from ALL 10 Points of Integration? Essentially, answering the questions you're about to read *is* playing The Integrity Game®! Master level players will not only have answers to questions from every set (bullet point) below, but will also work to make sure those answers "integrate" with each other so that the largest percentage of our daily activities (behavior) feed all 10 points of integration.

Here are the questions I ask my clients (individuals, teams, organizations) ... the questions I hold my clients accountable to having answers to ... the ten sets of questions Terry just asked of Luke ... who, like all of us, justifiably struggled with:

- **Meaning with Purpose:** Have you discovered or decided on what you believe to be a "meaning of life," and have you discovered or decided what you believe to be YOUR life's purpose? Are they integrated? Is there a clear connection between your meaning of life and the meaning of YOUR life?

- **Purpose with Gifts:** Do you believe, as I do, that all human beings are gifted, and have you decided or discovered what YOUR gifts are? Is there integration (a clear relationship) between your life's purpose and the gifts you've been given? Are you applying your gifts for hobby, pastime, playtime, or mission/service/ purpose?

- **Gifts with Potential:** Have you discovered or decided what your potential is based on the gifts you have been given? How many people you can teach ... how many books you can sell ... how many mouths you can feed ... how many kids you can put through school ... how many businesses you can start ... how high up in the company you can get? Have you declared what you are capable of achieving in the long term based on your gifts? Is there a relationship between your gifts and your potential? You bet there is!

- **Potential with Goals:** First of all, do you set goals? Chances are the answer is no because the Ivy League studies all conclude that only about 3 percent of our population sets goals. Second, if you DID set goals, would those goals be based on what you see other people achieving, or would your goals be INTEGRATED with YOUR potential based on YOUR gifts (versus what the Kardashians are doing, for example)? So many people are trying to achieve what others expect of them or what they see others doing, instead of looking within at the factors above and putting themselves in a position to be held accountable to integrity, but we're not done ...

- **Goals with Strategy/Tactics:** Do you have strategies to choose from that will help you achieve your goals? Are the strategies you are considering integrated with the goals you want to achieve? (If your goal is to increase sales and your strategy is to pray, I'm not sure there is ideal integration there. But if your strategy was to knock on doors and make phone calls, I think there would be more integration there.) Moreover, since there is more than one way to get a job done, are you considering strategies that are difficult or natural for someone (integrated) with your gifts?

- **Strategy/Tactics with Word/Commitment:** Have you selected a strategy and broken it down into the tactics (observable actions you need to take to execute the strategy), AND are you committed to taking that action? To whom, if anyone, have you shared that commitment ... given your word? What is your relationship with your word? Most people know that integrity has something to do with doing what you say you will do. So what percentage of the things you say you will do, do you actually do? And what percentage of the things you say you will do are integrated with a strategy or what you would call "strategic?" Legendary basketball coach John Wooden cautioned us not to mistake activity with achievement. Most people are really good at staying busy but what percentage of our day-to-day activities are things we said we would do, or strategic or advancing us toward our goals (which we probably haven't set) or our potential (which we probably haven't determined) or our purpose (which we are probably too busy to discover or too scared to acknowledge ... because as soon as we do, we can be held accountable ... I digress). Still not done!

- **Word/Commitment with Action:** We attempted to cover this in Chapters 5 and 6—are you making commitments to take strategic action toward SMAART Goals, and are you actually taking that action? Are you putting off or delaying the difficult things that you know will make the difference? For example, if we all did 100 things every day, how many of those 100 would be things we committed to doing ... things we said to ourselves or to another that we would do? Most people offer a number less than 50 percent when I ask this question in keynotes or group sessions. So, 35 percent of the things we do are things we said we would do ... but how many of the things we say we will do are tactics that execute a proven strategy for a specific goal? Now imagine me asking an audience to, "Raise your hand if you feel you have great integrity now?" Remember: please don't shoot the messenger; I'm not done.

- **Action with Growth:** Are you taking enough action to make mistakes? I ask because there is no such thing as a mistake—just learning and growth wrapped in a little discomfort. In fact, the only mistake to be afraid of is the one you don't learn from. Most people are so afraid of mistakes and failure that they never take action toward their goals as I've outlined above. So, I ask: are the actions you are taking integrated with your (personal, professional, financial, or spiritual) growth?

- **Growth with Achievements:** Straightforward, what are your achievements? Do you have any at all? Are they positive achievements or negative achievements? Getting locked up in jail eight times in eight years, for example, IS an achievement, but not one that is integrated with growth! What are your achievements and are they "integrated" (related) with the growth you experienced because you KNOW what you want and have COMMITTED to getting it? **And finally…**

- **Achievements with Contributions:** In our last point of integration, we "integrate" (come full circle) with the first point (meaning and purpose) when asking: what are you doing with your achievements … who are you sharing them with … who are you giving to … whose life are you touching with contribution … are you doing something that helps your family … that helps your community … that helps humanity? Is there integration between what you are achieving and who you are serving … who you are contributing to? Are the contributions you are making to this world integrated with what you believe to be the meaning of life and your specific life's purpose?

As briefly as I can ask to sum it all up: Do you know your *purpose, gifts, potential, goals,* ideal *strategies, capacity to commit, power of action, joy of growing pain,* the *responsibility of achievement* and *the personal fulfillment of selfless contribution?*

If not, that's okay. Luke didn't have all the answers, either, but look how well it turned out for him JUST from his willingness to be asked... to struggle ... to admit he didn't know ... to keep struggling and trust himself Sometimes, we have to see the ways that others believe in us in order to begin believing in ourselves. Nobody has all the answers, and nobody will succeed/find them alone. We MUST integrate with others, and I recommend they be people that see your gifts!

The first thing my brother did when he read the draft of this book is he texted me, referring to me as "Terry." He told me how obvious it was that I was Terry ... a little proud of himself for figuring it out, I'd add. What he didn't "figure out" and what I vulnerably share with you is that I was Luke before I knew I could be a Terry. Most important, I have a long list of "Terry's" in my life—people who believed in me more than I believed in myself, people who motivated me to PROVE THEM RIGHT—chief among them, my wife ... but there are others, like Dr. Mike Real, Dr. Peter Andersen, Jim Ristuccia, Bill Behrens, Dr. Richard Gerrero, and so many of my clients, colleagues, partners and friends. So many people have helped me believe in myself that I am forever committed to proving them RIGHT!

We have all had doubters and love proving them wrong ... this book is not about them! We don't achieve things with integrity when the "purpose" is to get back at someone or prove someone wrong. Our greatest claims to integrity are when the "purpose" is to GIVE back to the people who were right about us or who need a little bit of Terry in their lives to play/win their own Integrity Game!

So, no more underachieving. No more blaming others. No more procrastination. No more excuses and letting yourself off the hook! It's time to make "integration" your daily practice, and knowing what you want integrated is the first step toward claiming, earning, and having greater integrity! I hope this book has helped!

And *reading this book and answering the questions asked of Luke is a SINGLE-player game* ... which is better than not playing at all! But many of you may be asking "now what?" in search of additional ways to play!

-player game, with an *Integrity Game® Certified Coach*!

Some of you will want the *multi-player Integrity Game® Workshops and Retreats* for your teams/organizations.

Some of you will want a *Keynote Speaker who will be memorable, if not profitable*, for your audience and organization!

Others might want to play the *4-12 player version* by joining an *Integrity Game® Peer Advisory Group*.

Still, others might ONLY be interested in *"single-player" games, such as e-courses, self-paced online training, or info-products like this book and future editions*.

Some of you might want to *get Certified as an Integrity Game® Coach, Facilitator, or Trainer!*

Finally, *SOME of you might even want to co-author the NEXT version of the Integrity Game® with me* ... imagine featuring YOUR subject matter expertise in a new/customized parable that gets YOUR Integrity Game story told!

Through those options and more, it is my personal promise to help you apply what you have learned in this book to your life, business, career, family, or community.

While this book has come to an end, I assure you that the Integrity Game® has just begun!

All my Love and To Your Success!

Jeffrey Klubeck

JEFFREY KLUBECK

At the intersection of academia and business, Jeffrey Klubeck has applied his master's degree in Communication to over 20 years of experience in Organizational Development and Transformational Business Coaching. A coach before it was the trend, Jeffrey has had the opportunity to create performance management and talent recruitment frameworks with organizations such as United Health Care, JP Morgan Chase, State Farm, DOW Pharmaceutical, Altera Corporation, Tanner EDA, Aztec Shops, Ltd., Higgs Fletcher and Mack, LLP, Radiant Technologies, Chef Works, Inc., TGB Architects, Education Services District 105, and more!

With more than 3,000 learners and clients who have actively packed his courses in Public Speaking, Interpersonal, and Group Communication, Jeff's experience as a retired Professor of Communication has created a following of students and coaches who have been able to apply strategic critical thinking and paradigm shifts in their organizations.

Jeffrey has had the pleasure of speaking, training, and coaching on 4 continents to audiences from over 40 countries. Jeffrey's teaching, training, and coaching programs have been game-changing in helping executives, entrepreneurs, and business teams increase their motivation, accountability, and results!

In 2006, Jeffrey founded Get A Klu Inc. to offer coaching, consulting, training and speaker-for-hire services focusing on the "soft skills that make strong leaders." In 2019, Jeffrey cofounded, and by 2020 successfully sold his interest in, sideXside, LLC, which served as the parent company for the *Secret Knock, Prosperity Camp,* and *Mastermind Association* personal growth brands. From 2016-2018, Jeffrey was a regular contributor to Funnel Magazine and has also been quoted in more than two dozen Forbes Coaches Council publications since 2019.

Jeffrey founded The Integrity Game® in 2020 to offer keynotes, soft-skills workshops/trainings, executive/communication coaching to corporations and industry/trade associations. In 2021, Jeffrey was awarded the Excellence in Education Award by the Global Forum for Education and Learning.

Jeffrey lives in San Diego California with his wife of over 20 years Mary Ann, three kids (AJ, Abigail, and Brody) and two dogs (Bueller and Cookie).

Discover more and connect at:

www.theintegritygame.com and www.linkedin.com/in/getaklu/

Made in United States
North Haven, CT
09 April 2022

18015246R00078